OUT-OF-BODY

EXPLORING

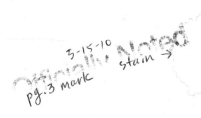

Also by Preston Dennett

California Ghosts (Schiffer, 2004)

Extraterrestrial Visitations (Llewellyn, 2001)

UFOs Over Topanga Canyon (Llewellyn, 1999)

One in Forty: The UFO Epidemic (Kroshka, 1997)

UFO Healings (Wild Flower, 1996)

OUT-OF-BODY

EXPLORING

A Beginner's Approach

PRESTON DENNETT

HAMPTON ROADS
PUBLISHING COMPANY, INC.
for the evolving human spirit

Cover design by Marjoram Productions
Cover digital image © 2004 Getty Images/PhotoDisc/Akira Kaede

Hampton Roads Publishing Company, Inc.
1125 Stoney Ridge Road
Charlottesville, VA 22902

434-296-2772
fax: 434-296-5096
e-mail: hrpc@hrpub.com
www.hrpub.com

If you are unable to order this book from your local
bookseller, you may order directly from the publisher.
Call 1-800-766-8009, toll-free.

Library of Congress Cataloging-in-Publication Data
Dennett, Preston E., 1965-
Out-of-body exploring : a beginner's approach / Preston Dennett.
    p. cm.
Includes bibliographical references.
ISBN 1-57174-409-6 (alk. paper)
1. Astral projection. I. Title.
BF1389.A7D45 2004
133.9'5—dc22

                                        2004013415

10 9 8 7 6 5 4 3 2 1

Printed on acid-free paper in the United States

Dedication

I would like to dedicate this book to you,
the reader, with a wish and a blessing
that you too will partake of the infinite joy, power,
and knowledge of the out-of-body experience.

Contents

Introduction

Every out-of-body traveler remembers when they first began going out of the body.

For me, it began on October 14, 1984, with a phone call.

I will remember that morning always. It was a beautiful bright sunny day. The Santa Ana winds had cleared the sky of the ever-present L.A. smog. I woke up in a fantastic mood. I turned to my sister Valerie (at that time we shared a bedroom) and remarked on how beautiful it was and how great I felt. She turned to me and said, "Me too!" We both thought that was unusual.

The phone call came when I was alone in the house. I was nineteen years old, the fifth of six children. In some ways, life in our house was just like the Brady Bunch, always bustling with activity. I couldn't believe I had the house to myself that morning.

I answered the phone, and a lady started to ask me questions about my mother.

"To whom am I speaking?" she asked.

"I'm her son Preston. Who is this?"

"This is Connie from her office. Do you know where she is?"

"Yes," I replied. "She's in San Francisco, at a convention."

"When did you last speak with her?"

"A couple of days ago. Is there something wrong?"

"How old are you?" Connie asked.

"Nineteen. Is there something wrong with my mother?"

There was no answer. After a few seconds, the reply came. "Your mother was found dead in her hotel room this morning. She died instantly of a massive heart attack."

In that second, my entire world shifted. My mother was dead.

I later learned the details. She had just taken a shower. She called room service and ordered breakfast. The heart attack came while she was blow-drying her hair. She was found lying halfway through the bathroom door reaching for the phone.

And so, at age nineteen, I had my first real experience with death.

Death is a strange thing. Sooner or later, we all die. And yet, we avoid the subject. Even when it strikes someone close to us, we avoid it. Now I understood why. It was too hard.

After getting over the initial shock, I realized that I knew little or nothing about death. I was sure, however, that there was no such thing as life after death.

Two weeks later, at the service, I saw my mother's ghost.

The service was being held at a friend's house. We all gathered to mourn and to give our last respects. As my father drove up in his car, I saw someone sitting next to him. As his car approached, I was wondering who it could be.

I got the shock of my life. There my mother sat in the front passenger seat, not ten feet away from me, as solid as could be. She sat poised, with her hands in her lap, just as she would normally. After a few seconds, she faded away and disappeared. Another family friend was sitting there instead, a black man. Not believing in ghosts, I simply assumed I was hallucinating. I told no one.

Acknowledgments

I have so many people I'd like to thank. First I would like to thank my mother for taking me on various tours into other dimensions. I would also like to thank my spirit guides, who have elected to remain anonymous, even to me. I'd like to thank my sister-in-law, Christy, for supporting me in my adventures. I'd like to thank the many teachers who have helped me along the way, including Robert Monroe, Bruce Moen, Robert Bruce, Robert Peterson, Stephen LaBerge, Samael Eon Weor, Jane Roberts, and the many other pioneers who have blazed a path into the unknown so that others may follow. Finally, I'd like to thank the Hampton Roads Publishing Company for being the world's leading publisher of out-of-body books. I couldn't have done it without them.

My ghost sighting became my dark secret.

As the months passed, our family settled back into its routine. I continued to attend college and worked part-time doing data entry. About a year and a half later, I had a second bizarre experience, which I classified at the time as a dream.

I See My Mother

I wake up (false awakening) when my mother walks into my bedroom. I sit up in bed, totally astonished. I am sure that I am really awake. I know instantly that this is really my mother. I tell her, "You can't be here, you're dead!"

She smiles and shakes her head gently. "It doesn't matter."

I am so amazed and happy to see her that we just hug. As we embrace, I can't believe how real it feels. Even though I know she has died, I am totally convinced that I am in her presence.

After a few moments, I awake. (April 1986)

As I lay there in bed, it took me a second to get my bearings. My mom was still dead. It had all been just a dream.

Just a dream . . . but it seemed so real. But it couldn't be real, because there is no such thing as life after death.

On some level, I was still convinced I had just been visited by my mother with an urgent message that there is life after death. But I just couldn't believe it.

My reasoning was simple. It can't be, therefore it isn't. And forget the fact that she came to me in a dream. Forget the fact that I saw her ghost. There is no such thing as life after death, period.

My mom, however, apparently thought differently, because it wasn't long before she visited me again.

It was the same thing. I woke up when someone walked into my bedroom. With a shock, I realized it was my mother. I was so excited to see her, I jumped up and hugged her. After a few moments, I woke up in bed.

Again, I told no one and just filed the experience in the back of my mind. However, as a result, I slowly developed an interest in the paranormal. I soon read everything I could about shamanism, UFOs, ghosts, channeling, dreams, life after death, and eventually out-of-body experiences (OBEs).

Intrigued by the possibility that I could have my own OBEs, I decided to give it a try. To my total shock, it worked. I soon began to have out-of-body experiences on a regular basis. After literally years of effort and practice, I eventually learned how to control the out-of-body state. As of this writing, I have had more than a thousand conscious OBEs.

I was delighted by these newfound abilities and felt like I had discovered a whole new world. Going out of body, I was able to explore not only the physical world, but the astral world. To my amazement, I found the astral dimensions to be an utterly real place, richly detailed and teeming with life. I expected to encounter glowing beings dressed in robes floating in mist. Instead, it was much more like physical life, only *more real.* There were buildings, oceans, forests, deserts, cities, and people . . . all much more real than I could have imagined.

By going out of body, I was able to fly to distant locations, visit the moon. I was able to take a tour of the heavenly realms and many different dimensions. I met with deceased loved ones, I rescued lost souls and I bathed in The Light. I explored my past lives, encountered my Higher Self, met my spirit guides, studied in the Akashic Library and traveled into the past and the future.

I wrote this book, the true story of my out-of-body adventures and explorations of the physical and astral dimensions, to inspire others to have their own out-of-body experiences. I'm convinced that if everyone had conscious OBEs, the world would be transformed. Therefore, various exercises are presented that teach not only how to go out of body, but what to expect once you get there.

Do we really need another book about out-of-body experiences? In most respects, my experiences match the experiences of others. However, several of the experiences I've had have not been reported by other explorers. The astral dimensions are truly an unknown frontier. There are very few recorded accounts of advanced astral travels. Our knowledge of the astral dimensions therefore remains surprisingly incomplete, especially when you consider how vast these dimensions are. Imagine sending twenty people to the planet Earth to explore for short periods. Likely, each would come back with widely varying accounts. Such is the case with astral explorations.

After having had extensive out-of-body experiences for nearly twenty years, I feel confident that I can offer some valuable information and insights into the nature of the out-of-body experience and the astral dimensions.

1

Early Out-of-Body Experiences

My first big surprise was how easy astral travel was. Once I started doing the exercises outlined in the literature, I immediately experienced lucid episodes: I was able to become conscious while asleep.

From the beginning, it became clear to me that out-of-body experiences and lucid dreams were inextricably intertwined.

The out-of-body experience (OBE) can be simply defined as a condition in which individuals perceive themselves as existing outside of the physical body. They report leaving their physical bodies during which time they are able to fly, walk through walls, visit distant locations. . . . The lucid dream can be defined as a dream in which the dreamer is able to maintain full waking consciousness and sometimes control the dream environment.

Most out-of-body explorers agree that lucid dreams are, in reality, out-of-body experiences. Some feel that they are an inferior form of OBE, others feel that they are superior. Some feel that they are the same phenomenon exactly, the only difference being the percipient's interpretation.

The main difference between the two, I think, is that with out-of-body experiences, you perceive the environment outside of you as being externally created and independent of mental influences. In lucid dreams, your environment is internally created, and is composed of mental projections.

However, this theory runs into a major problem, because as all out-of-body travelers know, the astral dimensions are *extremely* responsive to thoughts, and while out of body, it is very easy to slip into a finer dimension and create exquisitely detailed and lifelike mental projections.

In fact, as you advance with astral travel, it becomes clear that physical reality itself involves the same phenomenon of mental projections. Despite its seemingly fixed reality, the physical world is in fact composed of mental projections. Thus the concepts of internal and external become blurred.

Still, there are differences. I have had both lucid dreams and out-of-body experiences. I have astrally projected from a lucid dream, and I have had out-of-body experiences that evolved into lucid dreams. I have had out-of-body experiences that contain some mental projections, and I have had lucid dreams that seemed to be totally real. I have also had experiences in which I honestly cannot tell the difference.

As I became more proficient at out-of-body travel, I finally discovered why there is so much confusion. But in the beginning, I tried not to overanalyze my experiences and just went with the flow.

According to Robert Bruce, advanced astral traveler and author of *Astral Dynamics,* "A lucid dream is a genuine type of OBE, although the dimensional gate traveled through to achieve it is best thought of as being internal" (Bruce, p. 322).

Robert Peterson writes, "The scenery is 'artificial' in a lucid dream, but is 'real' in an OBE. . . . Regardless of what OBEs and lucid dreams are, I believe they are two separate phenomena. . . .

I do believe that occasionally people confuse one experience for the other, and granted, it's very difficult to tell the difference in some cases" (Peterson 2001, pp. 201–205).

William Buhlman writes, "One of the best ways to initiate an out-of-body experience is to become aware or lucid within a dream" (Buhlman 1996, pp. 27, 182). In fact, during an out-of-body experience, he was told that lucid dreams can be considered a higher form of OBE, as they take place in a higher vibrational dimension, meaning the astral dimensions.

Writes Vee Van Dam, "[A] lucid dream is the equivalent of a projection" (Van Dam, p. 68).

In any case, the two are so similar that it can be very confusing for the novice explorer. This was true in my case. Although I was able to initiate OBE's after only a few tries, attaining lucidity was a long and arduous process. Only by combining intense effort, will, and desire was I able to become lucid in the dream state. My early experiences were invariably brief, and I had little or no control over my actions. I had already had several lucid dreams before I had the following experience in which I moved beyond the lucid dream state and closer to the out-of-body experience.

Could I Be Dreaming?

I wake up, and it's completely dark. Not even darkness—I can't see anything at all. Nor can I hear or feel. I have no sensory input whatsoever. I am fascinated, and think, "Could this be a lucid dream?" As soon as I think this, I remember the rule, "If it could be a dream, then it is."

At this realization, knowing that I am asleep in bed and yet totally conscious, I become overjoyed. This is intensely different from anything I have ever experienced. Suddenly, I feel a wave of tiredness and start to lose consciousness. I recall that LaBerge [author of *Lucid Dreaming*] recommended spinning to maintain lucidity. So I try to spin. I feel a very peculiar sensation of a sideways spiraling motion, as if I were a washcloth being squeezed. I feel myself folding into myself, rolling and rolling, and then I lose consciousness. (July 31, 1987)

Finally, I was getting closer. I still was unable to maintain my awareness for any length of time. My experiences therefore remained brief.

Trapped in a Dark Box

I wake up from a dream. I realize that even though I am fully conscious and wide awake, for some reason I cannot see, nor cry out. I know I am lying asleep in bed, and yet I am totally awake. I realize I am lucid, and am fascinated by the feeling of having no sensations whatsoever. It feels like I am in a dark box (my body), but I can't feel it at all. After about twenty seconds, I wake up, amazed and excited. (November 21, 1987)

These two experiences are neither lucid dreams nor out-of-body experiences. I was neither dreaming nor was I out of body. These are the types of experiences the beginner can expect. If you keep up your efforts, however, you will be rewarded with something less ambiguous.

The following experience occurred immediately after I lay down on my bed during the day, just for a short rest. I consider it my first real OBE. I was 22 years old.

"I'm Doing It!"

Suddenly, I feel my body become extremely heavy. This is followed immediately by what feels like an electric shock pulsating through my body. I am totally unable to move or cry out, and my body feels like it's hollow and there is a waterfall flowing through it. It feels like I am touching a live wire. I recall Monroe's warning that you might feel a vibration. I'm thinking, "Vibration? That's the understatement of the year!" I'm sure I'm being electrocuted.

Suddenly, I feel a strange "whoosh!" I am up in the air flying. I zoom out of my bedroom, across the hall, and into the bathroom. I grab the counter and realize I am out of my body. I am ecstatic and say to myself over and over, "I'm doing it! I'm doing it!"

I feel a huge wave of tiredness sweep over me, and I fall back into a series of dreams. Upon awakening, I know that I have finally had a genuine out-of-body experience. (February 7, 1988)

Around this time, more and more of my dreams began to reflect physical feelings of heaviness or vibration. This feeling usually marked the early stages of an OBE. I wrote down every experience in a journal that I also used to record my dreams, which, according to many books on the subject, are often half-remembered OBEs.

"Hypnotized"

I am lying in bed, convinced I am awake. My sister walks in and says she's going to put me under hypnosis. I think she is being ridiculous. However, she starts saying, "You are getting sleepy . . ." when suddenly, my whole body, but especially my head, begins vibrating like I'm being shocked with electricity. I am unable to move and don't understand what is happening to me. I am convinced that I am already awake, and it never occurs to me that I am dreaming. (February 12, 1988)

Around this time, many of my dreams and lucid dreams began to exhibit strong feelings of sex. Later I learned that lucid dreams and OBEs are integrally related to sexual energies. At this time, however, I had no idea that sex would become such a big part of many of my experiences, so I was, needless to say, a little overwhelmed.

Someone Lies on Top of Me

I'm lying in bed with my blanket over my head when someone walks in the room and to my surprise, lies on top of my body. I am sure that I am awake, but for some reason I can't move. I am wondering who would crawl into bed with me and why. I feel a sudden wave of sexual energy, which becomes so strong I wake up. (February 19, 1988)

Although feelings of bodily heaviness are an indicator of an imminent out-of-body experience, it doesn't mean that you will have one. Often, I found myself rationalizing the feeling as something mundane.

A Heavy Weight

A sudden heaviness in my body wakes me up. I am convinced that I am awake in bed with my eyes closed. I can't understand why I feel so heavy, and I'm thinking that someone must be lying on top of me. I'm trying to think who would do such a thing. I try to move, but I am completely paralyzed. I struggle to break free of the paralysis until I fall asleep. (March 3, 1988)

Again, I failed to recognize the heavy feeling, and simply assumed that I was awake. Although I failed to realize that I was sleeping, I was in fact totally lucid.

I began to dream about eyes, usually with bizarre details or injuries. More and more mirrors appeared in my dreams, with my reflection being somehow different. This seemed to follow the same general pattern as OBE writer Patricia Garfield's. If you see your reflection in a dream, it is a sign that you have activated your astral double. Another dream cue that hounds me mercilessly is the appearance of celebrities.

Every week, another celebrity would visit me in a dream. I would always be shocked. And although I've had more than a hundred dreams involving celebrities, never once have I recognized this as a lucidity cue.

Nearly every dream contains bizarre elements which I believe are sent from one's Higher Self to ignite lucidity, to make the dreamer realize that he/she is dreaming. Recognizing these clues is a key to becoming lucid and then going out-of-body.

However, most of the time when I became lucid, it was spontaneously. I was now at the stage where I could transfer waking consciousness into the dream state. However, I was not able to gather my mental faculties to a degree where I could think critically. I continued to rationalize bizarre details—and to wallow in confusion when I couldn't.

My Alarm Clock Is Ringing

My alarm clock is ringing and wakes me up. I get up to turn it off, but for some reason, I can't seem to do it. I'm having trouble moving and seeing. Suddenly, I realize that I'm standing up in bed, and I can't seem to open my eyes. I can't believe what I'm doing, and I'm wondering what is going on. Why can't I open my eyes? Why am I standing in my bed? Why can't I move? I wake up to my alarm clock ringing. (July 20, 1988)

I continued to work on achieving the out-of-body state. This led to more and more bizarre false awakenings and confusing rationalizations.

I Fall Asleep on the Kitchen Floor

I wake up and realize with shock that I have somehow fallen asleep on the kitchen floor. My head is stuck under the bottom of one of the cabinets, and it takes me a while to pull myself off the floor and stand up. I finally do, but I am very disoriented and confused. I just can't understand how I could have fallen asleep on the kitchen floor. I can't seem to remember even going to sleep. I would never go to sleep on the kitchen floor.

Still confused, I walk back into my bedroom. I feel so tired that I can hardly stay awake. With a great effort of will, I am just able to make it into bed before I fall asleep. Instantly, I wake up for real. (February 9, 1989)

No matter how much I desired to go out of my body, I didn't seem to be able to do it at will.

I was still doing the various exercises. These included relaxation drills, visualizations, subconscious suggestions, and memory exercises. What worked best for me seemed to be a combination of intense willpower, desire, focus, and intent. Only by obsessing myself with the subject was I able to generate out-of-body events.

Out of Body!

I feel a huge flood of awareness. I am suddenly totally awake, and yet I know for sure that I am lying asleep in bed. I immediately surge out of my body. I am amazed at how easy it is. I am standing next to my bed, and I know for a fact that my physical body is still asleep. It is nighttime, and everything is very dark. Otherwise my bedroom looks normal. I'm having some trouble seeing, but my awareness has never been sharper. I know that I am out of body, and I am eager to try some experiments. I try to move, but feel like I'm trapped in molasses. I look around me and am shocked to see the figure of a man near the doorway. Although I can barely move, I am just able to reach the man. I grab him by the shoulders and shake him. His presence jolts my awareness and I am wondering if he realizes that I am out of body, or if he knows that he is. I shake him to try to wake him up. I am buzzing with excitement. I can feel chills racing up and down my spine and am at the verge of losing control of my emotions. I am just so happy to finally be out of body. The emotion is so powerful that I can't focus on anything else. I lose awareness. (July 15, 1989)

I had achieved the out-of-body state several times, but still had little or no control. I couldn't move. I couldn't see. I couldn't control my emotions. I felt like a child who had to learn everything from scratch. The process was slow and frustrating, but extremely exciting. To the chagrin of some of my family members, I talked of nothing else. I'm sure that they thought I had gone off the deep end. Perhaps I had, but I sure was having fun.

I wasn't at all surprised that some people had difficulty accepting these types of experiences. I could barely accept them, and they were happening to me!

Most advanced astral travelers believe that everyone goes out-of-body every night. At first this seemed absurd to me, but as I began to remember more and more of what happened to me at night, I realized it was true. We may think we are asleep, we may not remember, but the reality is, all of us are very busy every night. The following disconcerting experience made me realize that we do in fact go out of body every night; we just don't remember.

Out of Body and Scared!

I am suddenly conscious. I struggle to get my bearings. I feel like I've just woken up and I shake my head to clear my thoughts. I look around and realize I am standing next to my bed. My first thought is I must be sleepwalking. But I reject that theory instantly, because I am having a lot of difficulty seeing. Everything is very dark and blurry. I feel a wave of lucidity, and realize with a shock that I am out of my body. I am standing next to my bed, and looking down, I think I can just barely make out my physical body underneath the blankets.

I am suddenly overwhelmed by an awful wave of terror. I am mortally afraid that I have just died and will never be able to get back into my body. This is not so fun anymore. Totally freaked out, I dive back into my body. I feel a strange physical sensation of buzzing and stretching. The feeling gets very strong, almost overpowering, and suddenly, I wake up. (July 23, 1989)

As I lay there in bed, I had the strangest feeling that something very important had just happened. But even as I thought about it, I felt the memory of the event leave my mind. I was confused. What had just happened? Where I had just been? Why was

I lying awake in the middle of the night? I knew I had forgotten something, but what?

As if on cue, the memory of the event came rushing back to me. I was sleepwalking—no, I was in bed, but I was awake and standing. I was out of my body!

I was shocked to realize how close I had come to forgetting the whole experience, and it convinced me forever that there are a vast number of events that occur to us at night, and of which we have no conscious recall.

I am convinced that critical thinking is essential to becoming lucid and having out-of-body experiences. By keeping a constant awareness of where you are and what you are doing, you carry this attitude into the dream state, and hopefully not only remember what you are doing, but become aware of it while it is happening. For many people this is easy, and I did eventually learn how to do it pretty well, but at this point, I was still a beginner. Although I had experienced a few out-of-body experiences, most were still pre-lucid dreams, often with those pesky false awakenings, such as the following.

I Fall Out of Bed

Suddenly, I fall out of bed and wake up. I sit up on the floor in total confusion. I can't believe I fell out of bed. This has never happened before, and I know something is not right. Looking around me, I notice that my bedroom light is on. This is really wrong, because I am sure I turned it off. I never go to sleep with the light on. Suddenly, there are people in the room. Sitting up, I am shocked. This is not even my room! It is much too large. Who are these people and where am I? Didn't I just fall out of bed? I become increasingly confused until I wake up. (September 14, 1989)

I still have dreams where I repeatedly fall out of bed until I realize that I have actually left my body. I have to laugh whenever

I think that the main obstacle to becoming aware of our night-time adventures is that it never occurs to us that sometimes we are out of our bodies and dreaming. In the dream state, we hover outside our bodies and live our fantasies, or essentially our stream of consciousness. By controlling the stream of consciousness we can control the dream state. We stick in little cues, such as "I will remember everything that happens to me tonight" or "Tonight I will go out of my body."

At this point, I still struggled to understand the difference between lucid dreams and out-of-body experiences. Intellectually, I knew the difference. But when you find yourself floating out of body in a strange environment, it's a different story. I was so shocked that I found it hard to believe what was happening to me.

Most of my out-of-body experiences occurred early in the morning.

I Levitate

I am lucid. Looking around me, I am amazed at how real everything looks. Everything looks just like it does in real life. I wonder if this is really a dream, or if I am out of my body. I decide to go out into the living room. I am zinging with the nervous rush of energy and excitement that lucidity brings. I am in the living room. Everything looks totally real. I am amazed, and it suddenly occurs to me that maybe this really is real, and I am not dreaming at all! I am just barely able to shake off the doubt, and I convince myself that I am in fact out of body. I run through the glass back door and out to the backyard oak tree. I think, since I am out of body, I can fly. I jump up and land back on the ground. Again, I begin to wonder what I am doing. Could this really be a dream? Am I really out of body? It all seems so real.

But no, for some reason, I am sure that I am dreaming or out of body. I decide to try to fly again. I jump up, and this time, I levitate easily into the sky. I rise about twenty feet. It feels so great, I fly straight up as fast as I can. I know from experience that I have only seconds of consciousness left, and I am not about to waste any of these delicious moments of lucidity. I shoot straight out into space for twenty seconds, until I lose consciousness. Upon awakening later, I wonder how it is that I am always able to find my way back to my body. (October 21, 1989)

Other OBEers have noticed that feelings of lightheadedness mark the onset of an out-of-body experience. It was nice to know this when it happened to me.

Out of Body!

Suddenly, I am aware that I am feeling very dizzy and lightheaded. I am disoriented and wonder where I am and what I am doing. I realize that I can't seem to see clearly or hear anything. I feel increasingly dizzy until I am having a full-blown attack of vertigo. I feel like I am spinning around, falling, rushing. I realize that I am about to faint.

The feeling reaches a threshold and then I feel a sudden, pronounced swooping sensation. I find myself standing in the bathroom. I know instantly that I am out of my body. I am totally awake and standing in the bathroom, while my body is asleep on my bed. I am totally conscious, and know exactly what is happening.

I am having trouble seeing, but can definitely make out my surroundings. Everything looks normal, except for that eerie astral quality. I am very excited and eager to see if I can try some experiments.

I leap back towards my bedroom and am delighted by the way I move in a strange, floaty gait. Looking into my bedroom, I am shocked to see that there is a short man standing next to my bed. I grab his shoulders and spin him around to face me. Unfortunately, my vision blurs and I can't quite make out his face. As I struggle to improve my vision, I feel my consciousness slipping away. I try to stay aware and in control but it's no use. I feel my astral body lift itself up and float horizontally over my physical body, and plop back into it. I wake up with a snap! (December 8, 1989)

It took more than a year of trying before I learned to achieve the out-of-body state fairly consistently, at least three or four times a month. Unfortunately, nearly all of my OBEs were of extremely short duration. Staying out of body for more than two minutes would have been a great accomplishment. Going out of body is relatively easy. However, once you get there, you run into a number of other problems, including moving, seeing, thinking clearly, maintaining awareness, and controlling your emotions. After more than a year, I was still only at step one, getting out of body. The next steps proved to be much more difficult.

2

The Desire Body

The astral body is also known as the desire body or the emotional body. Once you start having regular OBEs, you'll know why. You will discover that every thought you have and every emotion you feel manifests instantly around you more vividly and powerfully than real life. Often, it becomes so real that you begin to doubt you are even out of body.

Writes Robert Monroe, "In Locale II [the astral dimensions], reality is composed of deepest desires and most frantic fears. Thought is action, and no hiding layers of conditioning or inhibition shield the inner you from others, where honesty is the best policy because there can be nothing less. . . . The raw emotion so carefully repressed in our physical civilization is unleashed in full force. To say that it is overwhelming at first is a massive understatement. In conscious physical life, this condition would be considered psychotic. . . . My first visits brought all the repressed emotional patterns I even remotely considered I had—plus many I didn't know existed. They so dominated my actions that I returned completely abashed and embarrassed at their enormity and my inability to control them" (Monroe 1971, p. 77).

Writes Albert Taylor, "I have found that during an OBE, emotions seem to be greatly intensified, almost as if I become the emotion itself. . . . The power of thought is a tool during the out-of-body experience that must be handled carefully and clearly. Remember, anything you can imagine you will see or experience" (Taylor, pp. 87, 99).

Writes Robert Bruce, "Fear, anxiety, anger, excitement, and the sexual urge—especially primal urges such as fear and sex—all have very strong emotional undercurrents that can cause particularly strong emotional feedback between the physical/etheric, real-time, and astral bodies. If not taken into account and controlled, primal urges can reflect back and forth, growing in strength and compounding. This can cause enormous problems for an unwary projector" (Bruce, p. 66).

Sylvan Muldoon writes, "Perhaps the most difficult thing of all to comprehend concerning the phenomena of astral projection . . . is that everything in the astral plane seems to be governed by thought—by the mind of the projector. As a man thinks, so is he! When I think of trying to convey just what this implies, I almost give up in despair and realize how insignificant is my ability to express myself. So I can only say again—as one is in his mind he becomes in reality, when he is in the astral body. If you ever learn to project consciously, you will be amazed at the response which follows your thoughts" (Muldoon and Carrington 1929, 1973, pp. 286–7).

For whatever reason, novice explorers have little control over their actions. Because thoughts manifest so quickly, the novice explorer often finds himself in situations both scary and amusing. I suffered badly from this. It's not easy to get used to the fact that you create your own environment just by thinking. And even worse, your thoughts are so immature and your awareness so tenuous.

Later I discovered that I was able to extend my experiences by first satisfying the appetites of my desire body. At this point, however, whenever my desire body got control, it went wild.

Also, as a beginner, I still experienced many lucid dreams that didn't quite cross the threshold to OBEs. However, I was learning how to gain control over myself while out of body.

Out of Body!

Suddenly, I am lucid. As usual, I react by becoming uncontrollably ecstatic. I feel my astral body zinging with powerful waves of energy. I leap up and start running as fast as I can. Everything around me looks gray and cloudy, but I can barely make out that I am running through the house at a weird angle. I am too excited to carefully observe my surroundings and just keep running until I lose consciousness. (December 28, 1990)

Every time I become lucid, I am totally amazed by the realness of the environment. There is always that moment of shock when you wake up and find yourself in a totally new state of consciousness.

Usually, when I have lucid dreams or out-of-body experiences, there is no obvious trigger. However, in the following case, it was critical reflection that allowed for the onset of lucidity.

Lucid!

I'm in my bedroom floating up and down. My sister sees me and is not at all impressed that I am levitating. I tell her, "Look! I'm levitating!" Suddenly, it occurs to me just how impressive levitating would be in real life. I couldn't possibly be levitating. I must be dreaming. The shock is intense as I feel lucidity rush into me. I become very lightheaded and feel goose bumps all over my body. The energy is too intense and I lose consciousness. (January 24, 1990)

The following experience is, I think, a perfect example why people find it so hard to tell the difference between a lucid dream and an out-of-body experience. I was out of body, but there were details in the experience that were obviously not real and were mental projections.

Out of Body in My Bedroom

I am walking around, feeling a little silly, because although I know that I am awake, it suddenly occurs to me, what if I'm not? What if this is all a dream? The realization is intense. Suddenly, I feel a huge rush of energy and lucidity. I become a little dizzy, but still clear-headed. I am having some trouble seeing, but I can tell that I am in my bedroom. Everything looks totally normal, and I realize I am out of body. Then, as if to challenge my assertion, I see a small card table in the center of my room. I know this card table does not exist in real life, and I become fascinated by its appearance. I run up to it. I suddenly remember, since I am in my dream body, I should by able to fly. I jump up, fully expecting to fly, but nothing happens. I jump up and down, trying helplessly to become airborne. For some reason, I can't seem to fly.

I look at the table and notice a stack of paper plates. I grab them and start throwing them like Frisbees. I am certain that I am out of body, and I am thinking that I can make these paper plates fly. To my surprise, they behave according to the normal laws of physics. I feel a twinge of doubt. Maybe I am actually awake? But no, I still feel that familiar feeling of lightheadedness with energy rushing up and down my spine. (January 27, 1990)

Various physical sensations continued to mark the onset of lucidity, including heaviness, vibrations, whooshing, stretching, lightheadedness. A new pattern that began was a feeling of intense thirst or a desire to eat. When I try to satisfy these urges, I am unable to do so. I may feel a mild choking sensation and then become lucid.

Out of Body

I feel an intense thirst. I go to the bathroom and bend over to take a drink from the faucet. The cool water flows down my throat. I am swallowing and swallowing, and the water feels so good. But for some reason, I can't seem to quench my thirst. I'm still incredibly thirsty and can't seem to stop drinking. The feeling of quenching my thirst becomes so intense, I suddenly feel a rush of lucidity. I straighten up in shock. I feel a huge wave of vertigo and my vision blurs. I recognize the sensations as being indicative of the out-of-body state.

Looking around me, I can see I'm in the bathroom. Everything is hard to see. I'm having trouble focusing. I look in the mirror, but don't see any reflection. Everything looks real and has the feeling of being real. I am excited to be out of body, and wonder what I should do.

Suddenly, my body lifts up and I float horizontally back into my bedroom. I am whirling in dizziness and trying helplessly to get some measure of control. I am unsuccessful and I feel myself pulled over my body and I plop back into it. I wake up instantly, amazed and excited. (July 8, 1990)

The real secret about the out-of-body state is the importance of memory. Believe it or not, we are nearly all in a condition of profound amnesia. We constantly forget who we are, where we are, and what we are doing. We lose hours and hours of experiences every night, and there is no reason to.

If you can hold on to your awareness continually, always keeping check on who you are, where you are and what you are doing, you are a perfect candidate for out-of-body experiences. Memory exercises are crucial to out-of-body experiences because you are *already* going out of body every night, you just don't remember.

Start now. Do you remember any dreams? Do you remember what you ate for dinner last night? Do you remember what clothes you wore yesterday?

The more you develop your memory, the easier you will find it to remember what happens to you at night. It will unlock not only the key to your self, but the key to other dimensions and even the future.

Nearly every dream provides cues to become lucid. It never

fails to surprise me the lengths to which my dreaming mind will go to rationalize bizarre information, to explain away the cue that is, I believe, designed to make me lucid.

A Bicentennial Penny

I'm in my bedroom when someone hands me a "bicentennial penny." I notice right away that although this penny appears to be a real penny, it is too big and too thick. I turn it over and am shocked to see the date: 1776–1976. I am a little confused, but decided that it must be a bicentennial penny. (October 12, 1990)

In the dream, it never occurred to me that the United States Treasury has never issued a bicentennial penny. Bringing awareness into the dream state, into your astral body, is a tricky process, especially because, in the beginning stages, you are in a state of constant confusion.

Usually, my OBEs occur spontaneously. As far as dream cues, I have to be hit over the head by a series of them before I will wake up to the fact that I am in my dreambody.

I Do Flips!

I'm looking at a computer screen and the characters are coming out all garbled (Cue #1). Then I notice that the screen is way too large (Cue #2). I get up and go to the bathroom. I look out the window and am shocked to see snow everywhere. It never snows here (Cue #3). Suddenly, I realize I'm dreaming. The scene dissolves.

As usual, I become overly ecstatic. Unable to control my excitement, I start doing flips like a gymnast. I can feel the rush of energy that is typical of the out-of-body state, and looking around, can't seem to see anything. (November 25, 1990)

My mind continued to experiment with different lucidity cues. One that worked was the appearance of an old friend from high school. Even though I was going out of body, it was clear that I was still in the very beginning stages of out-of-body travel.

I Meet John

I meet John, whom I haven't seen in years. I can't believe it's him and I wonder if this could be a dream. I instantly realize that I am in fact dreaming. I become overly excited and wake up. (December 22, 1990)

Karen Tries to Wake Me Up

I wake up (false awakening) because Karen is pounding on my door, trying to wake me up. She is saying something over and over again. "We are not ourselves! We are not us! We are not who we think we are!" She repeats this several times, punctuating each sentence by pounding on the door. She pounds so loudly I wake up. (December 27, 1990)

After I woke up, I was at first convinced that there really was someone at my door. It took me a second to realize that it was Karen, and that Karen wasn't in the house so it couldn't be her. Oh, it was a dream!

Around this time, another strange pattern began to present itself. Over and over again, I would become lucid inside a grocery store. Typically, my desire body would take complete control over my actions, and I would either destroy everything I could find, or stick it in my mouth and eat it.

In the Grocery Store

I'm in the grocery store and I see my father. His face looks strangely bloated. I am concerned until it suddenly occurs to me that I'm dreaming. I feel a rush of excitement, and unable to control myself, I start bounding across the aisles. I see my brother Steven, and I get a shiver of loneliness when I realize that they are not real people, but are my own mental constructions. Everything around me is a representation of my mind. I am alone in a vast universe of my own making. I am amazed, because everything looks so real. (May 26, 1991)

That was one of the few experiences where I became lucid because of a cue. Again, lucidity normally comes to me spontaneously. Or perhaps I simply don't remember the cue, and my memory starts from the point of lucidity.

In lucid dreams, I repeatedly have to convince myself that the environment is not real. Even when I know I'm dreaming and I know that the environment is fake, I still have a little trouble with the people. Like many novice lucid dreamers, I am still trying to wake up my dream characters.

"Victoria, I'm Dreaming"

I'm suddenly lucid. Looking around me, I see that I'm at work. I am trying to get over the shock of the fact that everything looks so completely realistic when I see my sister Victoria. I make a huge leap to her and pull her hair sharply. She looks at me with concern and says, "What's the matter?"

"Victoria, I'm dreaming!" I say excitedly. I want to convince her that this is actually a dream so she can share in my adventure. It doesn't quite occur to me that she is not real. (September 7, 1991)

One of the skills I had to learn in the out-of-body state was how to move. Most of the books say that you use thought to move. At first, I instinctively tried to walk, and this usually ended up with me leaping or floating off in an uncontrolled direction. Learning how to move took patience and practice. The less I thought about it, the easier it became.

I Fly Out of Body

I'm suddenly lucid. I fly quickly out of my body. I am elated. I fly out of my bedroom, down the hall, and into the living room. I am floating in the middle of the room, wondering what to do, when suddenly I lose the ability to fly. I crash to the ground and wake up. (September 28, 1991)

At age 26, I finally moved out of my father's house and into a condominium. I was also moving up in my career from data entry to bookkeeping and accounting. It was a big step in my life. I'll always remember that first night in my new home. On that night, I also had the following short OBE.

On My Balcony

I am suddenly out of my body, in full consciousness. I am standing on the balcony of my new condo. Everything looks totally real. (October 5, 1991)

I continued to focus more on going out of body and trying to maintain consciousness. This wasn't always easy.

Out of Body

I am suddenly out of body. I am totally disoriented. I feel very dizzy and start spinning uncontrollably. I fall to the ground and start crawling around on the ground. I want to see what it feels like to stick my body into something, and start looking for solid objects to put my body through. (February 1, 1992)

Around this time, the number of my OBEs increased dramatically. The only reason I could think of for this sudden increase was that I had finally trained myself to go out of body regularly. It had become a habitual action. Maybe it all comes down to the old adage—practice makes perfect. My interest in the subject often waxed and waned, and this could also be a factor. Whatever the reason, I couldn't have been more delighted. Finally, I had gone from crawling to taking baby steps. Now I was off and running. Still, I continued to be plagued by my usual obstacles.

Am I Really Out of Body?

I become lucid and leap out of my body. I am overly excited, and run out of my bedroom, into the living room, and then out onto the balcony. Everything looks totally real. I climb up onto the railing and prepare to jump off and fly, when suddenly I wonder, am I really out of my body? Looking around me, I feel a sudden wave of fear. What if this is real? What if I'm actually awake? If I was awake, I was doing something extremely dangerous. I could fall off my balcony to my death. I had better be sure that I'm out of my body before I jump. As I stand there, vacillating, balanced on the rail, I decide that I wouldn't be wondering about jumping unless I truly was out of body. I take the leap and jump!

To my shock, I fall three stories straight down into the bushes below. I am not hurt, but I'm a bit shaken up. I feel a wave of doubt, and lose consciousness. (July 12, 1992)

Out of Body, On My Knees

I'm lucid. I leap out of my body. I try to stand up, but don't seem to be able to. I fall to my hands and knees and start crawling around. I can't see very well. I'm looking for physical objects so I can feel what it's like to walk through them. (September 3, 1992)

My grocery-store fixation became firmly established with the following experience.

Lucid at the Grocery Store

I'm suddenly lucid. Looking around, I can see that I'm in the local Topanga Canyon market. As usual, I go wild and crazy. I start knocking things over, ripping apart packages, throwing cans across the room, breaking glass. I can't seem to stop and I don't want to. I keep destroying things until I lose consciousness. (September 11, 1992)

Later I would learn how to astrally project from a lucid dream. Although lucid dreams are fun, there is something about the OBE that feels more profound. It was relatively easy for me to have a lucid dream. However, the out-of-body state was much more difficult to achieve.

Out of Body

I am lucid. I can't see anything. I feel a strong buzzing vibration in my body, and decide to go out of body. I use the rolling method, and easily roll over and out of my body. The instant I am fully out of body, I feel a strong wave of tiredness and promptly lose consciousness. (December 26, 1992)

Maintaining my awareness during an out-of-body state continued to be my greatest difficulty. My OBEs were still invariably short and would occasionally evolve into lucid dreams. The following case was a consciously induced OBE that became a lucid dream.

Out of Body

I wake up in bed, turn over, and my body gets very heavy. I suddenly can neither move nor see. The powerful buzzing vibrations are pulsing through my body. My body is asleep, but my mind is totally awake. Suddenly I hear people talking outside my door. The noise distracts me. I think that the people are real. I lose my lucidity and think I have just woken up (false awakening). I get out of bed, go to the front door and look out the peephole. I say, "Hello out there!" and wake up. (January 31, 1993)

Patricia Garfield was a writer and lucid dreamer who maintained that she could astrally project from a lucid dream state. In her case, she would often project from a dream after passing through some type of physical barrier, like a closed door. This has occasionally happened to me, and is always a powerful experience. Projecting from a lucid dream continues to be one of the most common methods I use to go out of body.

Lucid and Out of Body

I am lucid. It is daytime, and I am walking down a pathway next to a steep hill. At the end of the path I see an old-looking, unfamiliar house with a cheap screen door. I reach the house and, on impulse, jump through the screen.

I pop out on the other side, feeling much more clear-headed and lucid and totally out of body. Looking around, I am surprised to see that I am in my dad's backyard. Everything looks vivid and real, but the lighting is strange, sort of dim with a subtle glow around everything. Everything feels very still, cool, and pure, but at the same time, alive and vivid.

I am totally amazed at this ability, and can't believe that my body is asleep in bed. I'm wondering if this is real, and I look for anomalies.

As soon as I look for one, I find it. I see my brother's dog Rouster chewing on something. I'm thinking he may be a projection.

Knowing I only have a few moments left, I stop gazing at the beautiful field behind the house, and start running across it with huge leaps and bounds. I start going faster and faster, leaping over bushes, and whizzing up and down hills until I lose consciousness. (February 15, 1993)

I usually become lucid spontaneously. This way, I seem to avoid the sensations of heaviness and electric-like vibrations, as well as the problem of trying to remain awake and fall asleep at the same time. Of course, I continued to have OBEs that were ignited from dream cues, as well as consciously induced OBEs.

Around this time, I began to do a lot of my astral projecting to the house where I grew up. Although I lived roughly ten miles away, I would always end up at the location of my childhood home. In fact, upon leaving my body, I would find myself in nearly the exact same spot, in the middle of my father's backyard.

I later learned the reason for this. According to Sylvan Muldoon, many projectors become lucid at the same area where they first attained lucidity. Writes Muldoon, "When you once become conscious in a certain place in the astral, you will probably become conscious in the same spot under similar conditions" (Muldoon and Carrington 1929, 1973, p. 193).

Robert Bruce reports that many of his OBEs and lucid dreams begin from one particular mall. Writes Bruce, "Your target dream scenario can be anything you like, but I strongly recommend a large department store or shopping mall scene that you know personally. For some reason, this scenario makes lucid dream projection much easier to achieve. I have no idea why this works but, what works . . . works (Bruce, p. 331).

The vast majority of my OBEs and lucid dreams begin from the same two spots, which just happen to be the locations of my first two conscious projections.

Almost Out of Body

I am in bed, trying to sleep. There is a kid knocking on the front door. Mudita, my niece, is also making a lot of noise in the living room, and I am angry because I think she's doing it on purpose. She knows I'm trying to sleep.

Suddenly, I feel a rush of lucidity. All the noises cease. I recognize them as "exit noises." I feel my body become heavier and heavier until it feels like I am being crushed into the bed. I don't seem to be able to get out of body, and begin to wonder whether I'm awake or asleep. (February 19, 1993)

Out of Body

It's daytime and I am lying next to my friend Hannah in my living room. She's lying on a bench and I'm on the floor next to her. Suddenly, my body feels that familiar heaviness. I am a little concerned because I think I'm awake, and I don't understand why my body feels so strange. I say to Hannah, "Oh, my body feels really heavy!"

She thinks I'm joking and starts laughing. Then she rolls off the bench and lies on top of me. She says, "Now, you're heavy!"

I feel a strange pop!, and I'm suddenly out of body, totally lucid. I feel a bit disoriented by the sudden change, and it takes me a second to realize where I am. Looking around I see that I am on the deck in my dad's backyard.

I am instantly entranced by the incredible beauty of the astral environment. Everything looks totally real, but somehow, it's even more vivid than real life. The grass is so green and thick, and I can see it so clearly. My vision also seems panoramic, as if my center of focus has expanded.

I am so excited to be out of body that I forget about any experiments I had in mind and just jump off the deck and start running through the field. I have some difficulty moving. I am halfway across the field when it gets too hard to move and I feel my consciousness swiftly slip away. (February 21, 1993)

Almost every time I go out of body, something unexpected happens. I've come to look upon it as one of the joys of going out of body.

Out of Body

I'm suddenly lucid. I leap out of my body and start running around my bedroom in uncontrolled excitement saying, "I'm lucid! I'm lucid!" Everything looks normal. I run through my bedroom door, through the front door, and into the hallway. I run through another closed door and jump down the staircase of my condo building. When I hit the landing, I sink through the floor up to my shins. I can't seem to get out. I laugh uproariously and am so amused by my bizarre situation that I lose consciousness. (May 16, 1993)

Am I Really Out of Body?

I am lucid and feel the familiar rush of cool energy. I jump out of my body and into the living room. I am shocked to see that all my furniture is missing and the room is nearly twice its normal size. I am not completely aware, and decide I better test to see if this is really a lucid dream. A bottle of shampoo suddenly appears in my hand, and I decide to squirt it all over the wall. As I rub it into the wall, I'm thinking, this had better be a mental projection; otherwise this is going to be a terrible mess. (August 2, 1993)

Out of Body!

I am suddenly out of body. Suddenly interested in the idea of going through physical objects, I stick my head through the closed window. I don't feel anything unusual. It's like it's not even there. (October 21, 1993)

Out of Body

I am lucid! I feel a wave of sexual desire. I reach out and grab a lady's breast. (March 16, 1994)

The majority of my lucid dreams and OBEs continued to take place at my father's house. I also continued to be bombarded with imagery involving mirrors and eyeballs.

Lucid!

I'm lucid. Looking around, it's daytime and I'm at Dad's house. I run into the bathroom. I am eager to see what my reflection looks like, as this has always proved interesting. As I gaze at my reflection, I am not disappointed. My face looks normal, except there is something very peculiar-looking about one of my eyeballs. It appears to be larger than the other, and the pupil is very dark and strangely dilated. (March 25, 1994)

I continued to battle for lucidity, and it remained very difficult for me to tell for sure if I was lucid-dreaming or actually out of body. My experiences were still too short and out of control to conduct any meaningful experiments. I was improving, but it was painfully slow.

Lucid

I'm lucid. It's daytime and I'm at my dad's house. I run into the kitchen and stick my head inside the cabinet. As I suspect, my head goes right through it without any resistance. (April 14, 1994)

At this point, one of the things I was baffled by was the fact that I was able to create environments that are totally unfamiliar to me. I can understand creating my own bedroom or a house I've been inside before, but often I create rooms that seem to be totally new to me. It is of course possible, however, that these foreign rooms actually exist and that I am visiting them out of body.

Lucid in a Hotel

I'm lucid. Looking around, I am shocked to see that I'm in an unfamiliar hotel room. It's very clean, sparsely furnished, and small. It looks like a Holiday Inn room. I am wondering if I'm out of body, or if this is all a projection. I feel myself begin to lose consciousness. I spin around and am able to maintain my awareness. The instant I stop spinning, I lose consciousness and wake up. (March 21, 1994)

Perception can be very difficult during an OBE, but when I've been able to maintain full awareness, perception is actually heightened. Everything becomes more vivid. Colors are more colorful. Textures are more real. Everything seems to glow and fluoresce.

Out of Body

I wake up because someone is lying next to me in bed. I am shocked. Who would climb into bed with me? I look and it's my coworker David. I realize that he's not real and I must be dreaming. I push him out of my bed. I leap up and look outside. There are Christmas lights everywhere. The colors are so beautiful and I am instantly entranced. I fly out the window to get closer.

Suddenly, there's a shift and I'm standing in my dad's bedroom. I fly out the window and land on the roof of the house.

It occurs to me that this is no longer a lucid dream. I am now out of my body and sitting on the roof of the house. It is bright and sunny outside, and very beautiful.

I sit there just drinking in the incredible peace and beauty of the early morning. After a few moments, I decide I'd better not waste any opportunities and, flapping my arms, I fly up until I'm about five hundred feet above the house. Then I swoop down at top speed. I see the telephone wires strung from the telephone poles, and I consider flying through them. I decide I don't want to be distracted by what it might feel like to fly through electric wires, so I fly over them.

I start doing loops over and around the house. I see a closed window, and fly directly through it. I note that there is no physical sensation whatsoever. This usually happens only when I have a very high degree of consciousness and know for certain that physical objects hold no barrier for the astral body.

I float down the hallway of the house. Whenever I feel a slip or dip in my awareness, I start chanting, "This is a dream! This is a dream! This is a dream!" Even though I'm convinced that I'm actually out of body and the environment is real, this "running commentary," as Robert Bruce calls it, maintains my awareness perfectly.

I am amazed to be lucid for so long. I look out the window, and it's still bright and sunny outside. I'm wondering what else I could do when I slowly lose awareness. I don't fight it and succumb to the feelings of tiredness. I wake up. (April 24, 1994)

One cue that constantly hounded me in my dreams is the ability to levitate. Over and over again, I find myself levitating in my dreams. Usually, I am totally convinced that I am awake and have somehow stumbled upon the secret of physical levitation. More rarely, I will realize the true situation, that I am dreaming.

I Levitate

I'm suddenly awakened from a sound sleep when I find myself floating over my bed. For a moment, I think I am actually levitating. After a short moment, I realize that I am lucid-dreaming or out of body. The shock makes me lose consciousness. (May 12, 1994)

My pattern of projecting out from within a lucid dream continued. As usual, I would end up in my favorite location, my father's house.

Attacked by Homeless People

I am walking down the sidewalk when I see a small group of homeless people. They are dirty, gaunt, and dressed in rags. They are also looking at me threateningly. Suddenly, they attack me. They are pushing, pulling, ripping at my clothes. I can't believe this is happening.

Suddenly, my brother Marco appears, turns to me and offers an explanation. He says, "Maybe you are dreaming?"

I look at him in shock. Of course!

I feel an extremely powerful rush of energy and lucidity. It's so powerful, it sweeps everything away around me. (September 13, 1994)

Lucid dreaming can be used to initiate OBEs, but it can be very frustrating to try and deal with the fact that you are essentially hallucinating. Even though I knew that my environment was a mental projection, like many novice lucid dreamers, part of me was convinced that I wasn't alone, and that the people around me were real. Because of this, I still repeatedly found myself trying to wake up my dream characters.

In my attempts to maintain control, I wondered if it would be possible for me to wake up if I needed to. I had never had this problem, but I figured it would be at least worth knowing. As I suspected, it was easy.

Out of Body or Lucid

I'm lucid. It's daytime and I'm in an unfamiliar natural environment. There are trees, plants, flowers, but I don't recognize the area. I am wondering if the environment is real or a mental projection. I fly around and land. I start touching the ground and plants. Everything looks and feels completely real. It occurs to me that this is not the way to test the reality of my environment. But the fact that I can touch the leaves makes me feel that this is not the physical environment as we think of it.

I wander around for a while, until I remember that I want to see if I can wake up. Usually just thinking of a desire manifests it, so I am surprised when nothing happens. I think, wake up, and still nothing. I start blinking my eyes open and closed, and after about three tries, I wake up. (October 21, 1994)

If you examine your dreams, you will see that most of them represent your fears and desires. By going out of body, you are forced to face these issues head-on. I was able to get over the fear barrier relatively easily. However, even late into my astral journeys, I continued to be overcome by feelings of excitement and desire.

I Meditate Out of Body

I walk into Dad's room and start touching the wall. It feels so real that I feel silly when I ask myself, "Could this be a dream?"

Then I remember that if you feel even the slightest suspicion that you are dreaming, then you probably are. I feel a huge shock and a massive rush of lucidity. I am dreaming and out of body.

I get overly excited and start to run uncontrollably. Then I remember my plan to remain calm, to maintain my lucidity, to meditate and carefully observe my surroundings.

With a great effort, I manage to sit down cross-legged on the floor. I look at the clock across the room. It says 9:00, or is it 3:00? I am trying to read it when I wake up. (November 10, 1994)

It took me a long time to learn control, but little by little, I moved past the lucid-dream barrier and increased the length of my OBEs. Going out of body is like learning to play an instrument, or performing a sport like downhill skiing or figure skating. It's really a matter of applied knowledge. You just have to learn how to focus your attention. As Robert Peterson says, going out of body is like walking a tightrope of awareness. It's not easy, but with patience and practice, it can be done. And the results are well worth the effort.

OBE at Dad's House

I suddenly wake up to find myself out of body in my dad's backyard. I am totally conscious. The air feels cool and everything is extremely serene and peaceful. I glide straight up into the sky until I'm hovering about a hundred feet above the house. I look around me, amazed by the clarity and beauty of the scene around me. Everything is crisp and vivid. I can see every blade of grass, every leaf, everything in perfect detail. It's absolutely crystal clear and so peaceful.

I am soaking up the tranquillity of the scene when suddenly there's a shift. I'm at the local market. Everything looks exactly normal, and yet I am certain that this is a mental projection. I react in a way that's totally uncharacteristic of me in real life, but very consistent in my lucid dreams. I go on a rampage and start tearing the place up. I pull products off the shelves and knock the shelves over. I crunch the boxes, throw cans, rip apart paper products, break glass bottles and totally devastate the place. I realize that my desire body has gotten control of me, but I can't seem to stop. (May 1, 1995)

I continued to practice movement. I have discovered that movement depends mostly on your level of awareness. When I am extremely aware, I have no problems with movement or moving through objects. When I do not have full awareness, I have problems not only moving through objects, but seeing.

Concerning movement though solid objects, Robert Bruce writes, "Most novice real-time projectors have some difficulty moving through solid objects like walls, doors, and windows, not to mention solid rock. Their belief system seems to play a large part in this difficulty. If they believe they can move easily through a solid wall or door and are willing to just do it, without even thinking about it, novices will be able to do so. If just believing they can move through solid matter does not work, it may mean they are not subconsciously accepting this ability. Awareness, effort, and willpower can be used to cover this" (Bruce, p. 350).

I think Bruce is correct; however, I also have come to believe that there are other factors involved, including the degree of vibration of your astral body. A few projectors (such as Sylvan Muldoon and Marilyn Hughes) claim to have moved physical objects while out of body, so clearly, physical objects can be manipulated and felt, or simply bypassed.

When I'm totally conscious, I often bypass any of the exit sensations, and simply leap out of my body. When I'm not, I experience numerous sensations like vibrations or vertigo. When I'm totally conscious, I have no problem moving through objects. However, I have never been able to affect the physical environment.

Awareness appears to be the key.

Out of Body and Flying

I'm suddenly lucid. I jump up out of bed and float horizontally over my bed. I turn over and can see my body lying in bed. I am out! I am amazed, as this is the first time I've ever seen my physical body from outside of it! I am sleeping under the covers. I can't see my face.

I start flying through the walls of the house and am shocked when I hit one of the walls, bounce off it and onto the floor. I shake my head in wonder. I know I'm out of body, and I can't believe that the wall seems so solid.

Not giving up, I fly through the other wall and outside. I swoop low over the rooftop, turning corners at nearly right angles. I am amazed and do this over and over again. I realize with delight that I can turn on a dime, and inertia does not apply in the out-of-body state.

I zoom instantly into fantastic accelerations and stop instantly with no deceleration. I keep practicing various movements until I lose consciousness and wake up. (June 10, 1995)

Out of Body, Over the Freeway

I'm dreaming when suddenly I become lucid. I feel a surge of energy and, unable to control it, I get overly excited and fly into the sky. I find myself flying over the San Fernando Valley. Looking down, I realize that I am zooming over the busy L.A. freeways. I smile, thinking how much easier life would be if we could get from one place to another through out-of-body travel. (June 24, 1995)

Out of Body, I Go to Another City

I wake up and realize I'm out of body. It's daytime and everything looks normal. I am still in the physical dimension. I fly higher and higher until I'm several hundred feet above the neighborhood, looking down at all the little houses and buildings. I fly forward, faster and faster, until everything becomes a blur.

I'm suddenly pulled to a near stop when I see a table stacked with various objects. I swoop down over the table and look at what's on it. I see an expensive-looking vase. I grab it and smash it to bits.

Looking around me, I see a wall. I float up and fly into it at high speed. I bounce off. I get up and try again, but bounce off again. After several attempts, I give up.

I start flying straight up as fast as I can. I feel a huge acceleration and suddenly, I'm in deep space. Everything is totally dark and I can't see a thing. I feel a flash of fear as I realize just how far away I am from my body.

I fly back down as fast as I can. Everything comes back into view. I land on the ground and try to walk. I find myself stumbling. I remember, "just think yourself where you want to go." I think myself forward and I am pulled easily forward with no hesitation.

I want to go up and try flapping my arms. This doesn't seem to work. Again, thought works best. I feel myself beginning to lose consciousness. So I command, "Take me to see John in San Diego."

I feel a whoosh and I'm suddenly flying over the city at huge speeds. I'm moving so fast that everything turns into a blur of color and motion. I become alarmed and disoriented, and instantly wake up. (July 4, 1995)

Moving while out of body continued to be tricky. Often I would find myself flapping my arms. This apparently is common with beginners. Robert Bruce admits candidly that he still uses this method. As he writes, "Learning to move while out of body can be a very comical process—in my early childhood experiences I always started by trying to navigate my way through the house to get outside. I would float and slide and blunder though the walls and usually end up getting stuck in the roof. Then, when I finally managed to leave the house, I'd skim along the road trying to get up enough speed so I could take off like an airplane or a bird. I would get airborne for a while by flapping my arms or using a swimming action (which really does help with flying), but could never seem to clear the surrounding trees and rooftops" (Bruce, p. 346).

I have to admit that often when I find myself out of body, I am so shocked to find myself flying that I automatically start flapping my arms in an attempt to stay afloat.

Out of Body, Flapping My Arms

I'm lucid. It's daytime, and as usual I am in my dad's backyard. I must be out of body. I start flapping my arms like a bird, and I rise slowly. I continue flapping vigorously and am just able to gather enough momentum to reach the top of the hundred-foot tall eucalyptus tree. (September 4, 1995)

I continued to be in a doubting state of mind. Every time I went out of body, I had difficulty convincing myself that I wasn't awake.

Lucid

I wake up next to Marco, his wife Christy, and our friend Elise. I start to tell them about my dream. Suddenly, I remember that they don't live with me, and there's no way they could be here. The scene sparkles into vivid clarity, and I'm suddenly at my dad's house. I feel a rush of lucidity. I realize that this is probably a dream, but everything looks so real. To see if I am out of body, I jump up into the air. To my surprise and delight, I float in the air.

I am dreaming! The strange shock of lucidity sweeps over me and I fly eagerly out of the house and down to the corner of the street. Everything looks so real, I begin again to think that I am actually awake. I start touching the plants as a sort of reality test. They feel real, but I am sure that I am projecting.

I walk down the road, alternately leaping and flying. There are other people here, but they don't seem to be able to see me. Again, I wonder, "Am I lucid-dreaming or is this real? Or am I out of body?" (October 7, 1995)

Although I was having multiple OBEs a month, I still had trouble controlling them.

Out of Body

I'm walking down the street when it suddenly occurs to me that I might be dreaming. I start running at full speed, and I feel the rush of astral energies. I keep running. Looking around me, I see it is bright daylight and I'm on Cheney Drive. Everything looks real. (October 26, 1995)

The constant dream cues make me think that my Higher Self is doing all it can to wake me up. It's almost as if another part of me has an independent awareness and is trying to help me. I wonder if my OBEs are generated by my own conscious will or if they are controlled by another aspect of my mind.

One problem that I find amusing but also annoying is dealing with the characters in lucid dreams. My main difficulty is that I know they are a projection of my own psyche, and according to popular dream theory, represent an aspect of myself. This fact becomes especially irritating when my dream characters start laughing at my weak efforts to remain lucid.

Out of Body, Out of Control

I think I'm awake, lying in bed. I wonder what time it is. I look at the clock, and it says 8:15 A.M. It occurs to me that it couldn't be that late—I must be dreaming. I feel a strong rush of lucidity and a whooshing feeling. I am suddenly standing in my dad's living room, out of body. It is daytime.

I can feel that I have a loose grip on consciousness and will probably be awake for only a few seconds. In order not to waste any precious time, I run towards the back door and try to fly through it. To my shock, the door is totally solid, and I bounce off it.

I see Marco standing outside watching the whole incident. He thinks it's all terribly funny and laughs uproariously. (February 26, 1996)

While most of my OBEs occurred spontaneously, I have also been able to induce them consciously, as in the following experience.

A Consciously Induced OBE

I wake up in bed, and since it is still early, I decide to try to go out of body. I lie back in bed and watch the thoughts in my head. At first they are vague, fleeting images. Suddenly, however, I find I am standing in an unfamiliar parking lot. This is a lucid dream. I feel a bit of a shock because seconds ago I was lying in bed, and now I'm outside and standing up. I can't feel my body at all. I try to move and this creates a weird, uncontrollable twisting motion. Everything turns pitch black, and all my efforts to see fail. I can feel my body swirling and flying around uncontrollably. I am out of body, but I can't maintain it. I fall asleep and wake up. (March 17, 1996)

By this time, I was beginning to have some pretty advanced OBEs. Nevertheless, I still found myself struggling to remain conscious.

Out of Body

I'm lucid. Of course, I'm at my father's house. I fly outside and above the house. Not sure if this is a lucid dream or an OBE, but it sure looks real to me. I fly around the house three times. I think about flying through the power lines, but decide to avoid them. I keep flying around, swooping and doing twirls until I lose consciousness. (July 29, 1996)

Around this time, I began to receive more and more evidence that my out-of-body experiences were real and not lucid dreams. For example, in November of 1996, I traveled to Las Vegas to speak at a convention.

That night, in my hotel room I had the following brief OBE.

Out of Body Over Las Vegas

I'm lucid. I fly out of my body, through the ceiling of the hotel room and up over the building. It's early morning and everything looks bright, sunny, and clear. I flap my arms and am able to climb several hundred feet in the sky. Everything looks totally real. The view is fantastic. I'm examining the city of Las Vegas from an unbelievable vantage point. I recognize the buildings and am convinced I am totally out of body. I lose consciousness and wake up. (November 10, 1996)

Even late into my astral travels, I continued to become lucid at my father's house. While most of my OBEs remained brief and littered with mental projections, I was beginning to have longer and longer experiences that appeared to be genuine OBEs. It is a strange feeling to be walking around and be totally invisible to people. If people knew what was going on all around them in the invisible world, they would be shocked.

Out of Body in San Diego

I'm sleeping in the living room at Jon's house in San Diego. He comes out of his bedroom and says, "Preston, wake up!" and starts to poke me. I am annoyed and tell him, "No, let me sleep, I'm too tired." I am so tired that I can barely speak. My eyelids are so heavy, opening them is out of the question. I hear him making coffee. Two children enter the room and he accidentally burns them. I get up to help Jon pour cool water on their burns.

Suddenly, there's a shift and I'm back in my condo in Los Angeles. I lie down and pretend to fall asleep. Suddenly, I'm lucid. I pop out back in Jon's living room in San Diego. I am out of body and totally conscious and in control. The feeling of peace is delicious.

I slide out the window and decide to do some exploring. I float lazily above the sidewalk down the street towards the ocean. It is early morning and many people and cars are passing back and forth. This is incredible. I fly back and forth in front of people on the sidewalk, but they don't see me. They don't react to my presence at all. I fly down and land right in front of a young man with brown hair, a denim shirt, and jeans. I'm waving my hands and shouting at him, but he doesn't react at all.

I grab him by the belt and let him drag me along the beach after him, as if I were a helium balloon. I am laughing because he has no idea that he has just taken on an extra passenger. I feel a tug and am pulled back into my physical body. (March 8, 1997)

Out of Body

I wake up feeling very relaxed and decide to try and have an OBE. I close my eyes and relax my body, and allow myself to kind of let go and drift off. Almost instantly, I tune into the vibrations which quickly become stronger. I hear what I've come to recognize as "exit noises." This time it sounds like there are people talking in my room. I roll out of my body and start flying through my room. I do a couple of circles around the room and then apparently I get too close to my body because I fall back into it.

I turn over, relax, and tune into the vibrations again. My whole body goes completely numb. Suddenly Valerie and Dad are in my bedroom. How did that happen? They don't live here. Then I realize what's happening. More exit distractions. That means I'm ready to go. I roll out of my body and fall to the floor. I dart to a standing position. I start flying around, but I can't seem to see very well.

I remember my plan to first increase awareness and then obtain proof that I'm actually out of body. I shout out, "Increase awareness!" over and over until I feel my consciousness become nearly as sharp as it is in the waking state. I'm still having trouble seeing, so I shout out, "Clarity!" My vision slowly clears. Looking around me, I see that I am in an unfamiliar room. I remember that you can transform a lucid dream into an OBE by going through a barrier. I fly through a wall and pop out the other side.

I'm floating over a field or parking lot. Is this the parking lot to the mall near my condo? I can't tell for sure, but I think so. It's very bright and sunny. I fly down through cars and people. Nobody can see me. I fly around people, circling them and trying to get their attention, but I'm totally invisible. I look down at my body. I'm wearing clothes and shoes.

I fly up, up, up until I'm maybe two thousand feet above the San Fernando Valley. I look down at the landscape. I see dots of cars, buildings, people, the lines of streets. I feel a little nervous about how high up I am. I'm glad I'm out of body because a fall from this height in the physical would be fatal.

I dart back down like a missile. I'm back over the parking lot and I'm trying to get people to notice me. I fly back and forth in front of them, but I'm like a ghost. I reach out and grab a man's belt. I'm laughing and wondering what he would do if he knew I was there.

I'm feeling pretty confident that he's a real person and I'm actually out of body and not lucid dreaming. Just to be sure, I fly upwards and spin several times to erase all illusions. Unfortunately, the effort consumes my awareness and I fall asleep and wake up. (May 4, 2002)

Maintaining awareness while keeping my thoughts and emotions under control proved to be my biggest obstacle. But I finally reached the level where I could initiate an out-of-body experience and maintain the fragile state of awareness for at least a few minutes. I learned the hard way to keep my mind free of thoughts and emotions, thus protecting myself from falling into a lucid dream. I learned how to move and to see. Finally, I evolved to the point where I could do some real exploring. Now I had the ability to control my OBEs. The real fun was just beginning.

3

Experiments on the Astral Plane

As time went on, I began to really progress in my attempts to go out of body. Although it took years, I finally reached the point where I could produce out-of-body experiences on a regular basis. I finally learned how to not only initiate lucidity but maintain the fragile state and start doing the experiments that I had read about. Finally, after all that meditation, self-hypnosis, mantra-chanting, suggestion, willpower, and exercise, I was able to start some serious research.

Although I was still only taking baby steps, each lucid dream or OBE taught me something new.

I had already walked through walls, looked in the mirror, flown around, examined my surroundings, and experimented with numerous body-sensations including heaviness, thirst, choking, lightheadedness, vibrations, rushing, whooshing, stretching, and sexual arousal.

Now I could begin to explore the physical world. I soon learned that this was easier said than done.

The problem is that when out of body, it is very difficult to stay in the physical world. The natural tendency is to slip into the astral dimensions. Writes Robert Monroe, "The Second Body is basically not of this physical world. To apply it to visits to George's house or other physical destinations is like asking a diver to swim down to the ocean bed without scuba gear or a pressure suit. He can do it, but not for long, and not too many times. . . . Thus travel to points in the physical world is a 'forced' process in the Second Body state. Given the opportunity of the slightest mental relaxation, the Supermind will guide you in your Second Body into Locale II [astral dimensions]. It is the 'natural' thing to do" (Monroe 1971, p. 76).

Again, I think this is where much of the confusion between lucid dreams and out-of-body experiences lies. While out of body, you quickly leave the physical world and enter the astral dimensions, where your thoughts instantly manifest.

My next experience taught me well the difference between lucid dreams and OBEs, how the lucid dream is created, and the amazing properties of the astral plane.

Out of Body and Creating Objects

I am suddenly conscious. I know that I am in bed asleep. I'm not dreaming and am surrounded by darkness. I am delighted and amazed at how clear my consciousness is. Normally I have to cling to consciousness. This time, I have a strong grip on awareness. I decide to practice my astral vision. I think of an apple and try to create an image of it in my mind. In a flash, I see an apple floating in front of me in perfect form. I examine the apple, amazed that my mind could create something so realistic.

Feeling bold, I decide to try something bigger. I think of our garage, and it builds up rapidly around me, like a high-speed watercolor painting. After a few seconds, it coalesces and becomes pristinely real. I look around me, again astounded by how realistic everything is.

I go crazy and start manifesting everything I can think of. I make trees, cars, buildings—anything and everything that comes to mind. Everything looks completely real, virtually indistinguishable from real life. The only difference I can detect is that everything on the astral plane is more vibrant, more colorful, almost glowing. (December 9, 1990)

This experience proved to me that the astral plane is composed of a material that responds to our thoughts. This is why occultists are so fond of saying that "thoughts are things." When we dream, we are really out of our bodies on the astral plane, manifesting our thoughts and playing out personal dramas created by our minds. In the lucid-dream state, we become aware that we are in fact manifesting our thoughts, and we can manipulate the dream state, thereby exploring the inner world. The out-of-body state is the flip side—you explore the outer world. On the astral planes, this would equate to "consensus realities," where multiple people experience the same environment.

The main problem is, when we are out-of-body, it is hard to see past the illusions created by our own minds. Once we do, we can obtain verified details of the physical world, thereby proving that the out-of-body experience does take place in objective reality.

The point is, lucid dreams and OBEs are closely related, but definitely different phenomena. This becomes especially clear when the lucid dreamer projects out of body from the lucid-dream state.

Out of Body

I'm suddenly lucid. I slide smoothly out of my body and off the bed. I am totally blind. I decide to practice my astral vision. I think of the color orange, and it appears all around me vividly. Then I think of words, and I see them coalesce in front me, as if on a giant page. Suddenly, images are flooding around me.

There are plants and grass and trees. I'm in nature. (August 17, 1991)

One experiment that I've always wanted to try was to see if I could use my voice while out of body. When I finally remembered to try the experiment, I was not disappointed.

Out-of-Body Singing

I'm suddenly awake and out of body. It is totally dark. I can't see a thing, but I know I'm out of my body, in my bedroom standing near my bed. I decide to see if I can sing the scale. I sing out loudly, Do-Re-Me-Fa-Sol-La-Ti-Do! It sounds great. I sing it again. I feel proud to have achieved my goal. (August 31, 1991)

Being unable to maintain the out-of-body state was beginning to get frustrating. But like all things, with practice I became better. I had finally reached the point where I could maintain the state long enough to at least attempt experiments. Although my experiments weren't always successful, the results invariably taught me something. And with persistence, I was usually able to succeed.

Experimenting on the Astral Plane

Suddenly, I am lucid. I leap out of my body and stand up. I am in my bedroom and everything looks normal. I am very excited. I rush out of my bedroom and end up inside a strange room I don't recognize.

I look around me. I appear to be inside somebody's house, but I know that despite how real it looks, it is all probably a mental projection. I see a door. I recall one of the experiments that I wanted to try, which was to make love on the astral plane.

Looking at the door, I say, "Behind this door will be the person I most want to make love to."

Envisioning a gorgeous blond, but not really knowing what to expect, I fling open the door. I am shocked at who I see. It is an older lady that I had just recently met. I was not sexually attracted to her at all, but I had to admit that in real life, I was very fascinated by her. Still, this was not what I had expected.

Disappointed by the result of this experiment, I turn away. The shock nearly costs me my lucidity. To maintain awareness I shake my head back and forth, then fly into the air and start doing loops. It works perfectly. Looking around, I see I am in the same room, but I am now standing in front of a large glass window.

I decide that this would be a good opportunity to test how the environment of the dream state reacts. Knowing I can't hurt myself, I crash my fist against the glass. The window only cracks slightly. I smash my fist against it a second time, and the glass cracks into a frosted spider-web pattern. I smash the glass a third time and it shatters outwards. As the glass breaks, it makes very little noise and behaves almost like hard plastic. I pull the remaining shards out of the frame and look outside.

There is a normal-looking sidewalk along the side of the house. I see a narrow strip of soil next to the house. Amazed that I am still lucid, I decide to try another experiment. I have never heard of anybody smelling in a lucid dream, so I bend down and sniff the ground. I am delighted when I smell a subtle odor of moist earth. Although the scent is faint, it is definitely there.

I feel a wave of excitement that I was able to complete the experiment, and I decide to celebrate by flying. I fly out the window and start doing loops and swoops through the sky until I lose consciousness. (March 8, 1992)

Reading is supposed to be extremely difficult while out of body. During one of his OBE forays, Robert Monroe attempted to read an astral book. As he writes, "I thought of trying to see the title on the end of the book, and promptly the end was held for me to see, but the print was too small, or I was too myopic. Try as I might, I could not read it. Finally, I gave up, and the book was opened and I saw both printed pages. Again, I tried to read it, but it was just out of focus. Finally, I mentally suggested that I might be able to read it if I took one letter at a time. In response, a letter jumped out of a line and I just barely saw it as it flew by. I checked and rechecked carefully and laboriously, and got four words: 'Evoke unhappy beings by . . .' I tried to read more, but evidently I concentrated too hard, as it only became more difficult" (Monroe 1971, p. 134).

However, several people have been able to successfully read long messages in dreams and there is compelling evidence that many works of literature are first written in the higher dimensions and then translated into the physical dimension. Jane Roberts claims that many of her books were already written on the astral planes and she simply translated them. Robert Moss has also been able to translate long dream passages into the physical world.

My own experiments with reading have been mixed. On occasion, I have been able to produce extremely vivid hypnogogic imagery of writing. I have also had many lucid experiences where I am reading long passages of writing that seem to make sense while I am reading them, but I can't seem to translate them into conscious memory.

I was eager to try more experiments in this area. My first attempt started with a lucid dream reading experiment and ended in a full-blown astral projection.

Out of Body

I'm talking on the phone with Jack. I hang up and walk to another room. Looking around, I'm wondering where I am. I don't recognize the house, but it looks like my father's friend Diane's old house. There are shiny wooden floors and a long staircase going down.

I sit down on the ground and start playing with a plastic package of sour cream. I roll the package back and forth when it suddenly starts to accelerate by itself. I instantly recognize the anomaly as a dream cue and become lucid.

As usual, I am totally astonished. I feel a huge rush of energy and excitement, and I feel a strong urge to jump up and fly out of control. I remember that this usually causes me to lose awareness, so with a great mental effort, I force myself to sit down and remain calm. To help maintain my awareness, I remind myself over and over, "I'm dreaming! I'm dreaming!" I am amazed at how well this works and my thinking becomes clearer and clearer.

After a few moments, I feel I have a strong enough grip on consciousness to try some experiments. I remember that I want to try lucid reading, so I grab the sour cream package and read the words on the side. I laugh because the words are ridiculously small and very hard to focus on. With a great effort, I attempt to focus in on one word. Just when the letters come into focus, they dart back and forth, and start transposing as if avoiding my direct gaze. Not wanting to waste any more moments on something that wasn't working, I set the package down and look around for something else to do.

I am still in a strange home, and I am amazed at how real everything looks. I have never seen this room before, and it's hard to believe that it is manufactured from my own mind. I wonder what it looks like outside. I get up and walk/float to the window. To my shock, there is another person outside, floating a few feet off the ground.

Amazed that I am not alone, and wondering if this is a real person, I leap through the window screen towards the person. I feel a slight resistance as my dream body passes through the screen. It is a peculiar sensation, and I can feel the screen tugging at the inside of my body as it passes through the screen.

I am thrust out on the other side with an almost audible pop, and I am incredibly lucid and totally out of body. I am floating weightlessly and don't seem to have any physical form. I am in a place with lots of light and fog. It looks featureless, and I have the strong sense that I'm no longer in the physical dimension, but in the astral dimensions. I feel a strong vibration of positive energy that puts me into a delicious state of consciousness.

I am reminded that Garfield said that lucid dreams can turn into out-of-body experiences, especially by passing through a barrier. I am amazed at how accurate she is. I remain floating there in this exquisite state of pure consciousness for a few moments. Without warning, I lose awareness and wake up. (March 3, 1993)

Lucid Reading

I'm lucid and in an out-of-body state. I am in the place where I can create objects just by thinking about them. I decide to see if I can read. Suddenly I can clearly see words. I am reading them, and the letters are staying in place, but I can't seem to remember what I'm reading! (February 13, 1994)

Another Lucid Reading Attempt

I'm lucid. I decide to attempt reading. A notepad dutifully appears in my hand. I read it and am shocked to see a sequence of letters and numbers in perfect detail. Unfortunately, they are random and make no sense at all. Just in case, I try to memorize them. It reads, A-T-V-0-10-B-C-4-T, or something like that with dashes between each character. I am simultaneously amused and disappointed. (July 9, 1996)

I used to think of the astral world as being made up of only energy. This may be true, but I am continually surprised by how *physical* events feel. In the astral world, we are able to duplicate any experience we have on earth. The material of the astral world seems to conform to our thoughts, and we create and project utterly convincing environments. In fact, we are so good at this that most people never even consider that what they see around them is merely a projection, and this of course, remains the single biggest obstacle in becoming lucid and going out of body.

However, when you become aware that you are out of body, the fun begins. Assumptions that everything is real go out the window, and you are free to explore the astral environment in a more objective manner.

One of my major questions was just how real the astral plane was. My experiments pretty much confirmed my suspicions: The astral plane can feel just as physical as the physical plane.

Astral Matter

I'm in my bedroom when I suddenly become lucid. I remember my desire to test how physical the astral world is. Looking ahead of me, I see a typewriter on a table. I laugh because I do a lot of typing at work, and I don't really want to do it unless I get paid. Rushing with that strange cool energy and excitement that is unique to lucidity, I run up to the typewriter and begin typing furiously. The typewriter works perfectly and behaves exactly as it would in real life.

I feel the keys, and they are hard and smooth. I grip the side of the typewriter, and feel the texture of the hard plastic. I can't believe how solid and real it feels. I am amazed at the skill of my subconscious to be able to fabricate something so detailed and physically real. My dream typewriter is indistinguishable from a physical typewriter in every respect. I can see why many out-of-body explorers believe that everything in the physical world has its origins in the astral world. (March 10, 1993)

I have often wondered if my body actually vibrates when I go out of body. Once you feel the unbelievable strength of the vibrations, you'll know what I mean. If someone were watching me physically, would they see anything? If I shout in a dream, does my physical voice make a noise?

All these questions were answered in the following experience, in which I was able to consciously enter the lucid state.

Lucid!

I am lying awake in bed with my arm over J—'s stomach. I feel very relaxed when suddenly my body feels very heavy and starts to buzz violently. I recognize the sensations and realize I am ready to go out of body. As if a switch were flipped, I lose all bodily sensations. I know my body is asleep in bed, and my arm is draped over J—'s stomach; J— is awake.

I find myself in a desert environment. I recognize it immediately as Wickburg, Arizona, where we recently camped. I am looking around for a contact lens. Finally, I find it.

Amazed that I am still lucid, I begin to wonder about my body. I know that J— is awake and lying next to me. I wonder if it would be possible for me to communicate. I desperately want J— to know that even though I appear to be asleep, I am totally awake. I am concerned about the fact that I am out of my body while touching someone else who might accidentally wake me up.

I shout out loud, "J—, I'm dreaming! J—, I'm dreaming!" I can barely get the words out, but I can clearly hear my voice. After a few more repetitions, I bring myself back to waking consciousness. (March 21, 1993)

I sat up in bed and asked J— if my body moved or if I said anything. The answer to both questions was no.

I continued to become lucid regularly, and I was able to conduct more and more experiments. I hadn't seen my mom in a while, or at least I hadn't remembered it, and this was the main reason I wanted to learn out-of-body travel. Although she had come to visit me, I wanted to go visit her.

I decided that this would be my next experiment.

Lucid, I Call for Mom

I'm lucid. It's nighttime and I'm on an unfamiliar city street. I know for sure that I am lucid-dreaming. I can feel the familiar rush of goose bumps, and to maintain my consciousness, I repeat over and over again, "I am dreaming." Feeling a strong hold on awareness, I decide to call for my mother. I shout out, "Mom!" After about a second, I hear my voice echo all around me from everywhere at once. My voice sounds strange and muffled.

I try to call out again, but can't seem to speak. Looking around me, I see a storefront. I walk in, and I see my sister Victoria and a few other customers. I rush up to them and say, "Do you know I'm dreaming?"

They don't seem convinced. I think, "Poor people, if only they knew this was all a dream." I am amazed that I am still lucid. I am wondering what to do next when I feel my awareness fade. I fight to stay conscious, but it's no use, and I fall asleep and wake up. (March 9, 1994)

I have found that while I am out of body, my longest and most profound experiences occur when I am task-oriented. If I achieve the out-of-body state and don't have a plan, I immediately become overwhelmed with excitement and lose all control.

Robert Bruce advises, "Plan projections and get into the habit of sticking to your plan. Have primary, secondary, and tertiary mission goals, and focus on these during projection. . . . Apart from making projections more productive, this also gives the projected double something definite to focus on during each OBE" (Bruce, pp. 311–12).

If I have plan or a goal, I can focus only on it and thereby keep control of my emotions and maintain awareness. The more focused I am on my task, the easier it is to achieve. For some reason, however, when I am out of body I am, like a small child, easily distracted.

I wanted to get conclusive proof that I was out of body. My plan was to go to my brother's house and observe details that I could not know in waking life. It seemed like a relatively easy task. Easy in the physical, maybe.

Out of Body, in Search of Proof

I'm walking down an unfamiliar city street when it suddenly occurs to me that I am dreaming. I start running and leap into the air. I fly effortlessly into the sky. I feel a buzzing rush of energy. The environment around me suddenly flashes into an almost surreal vividness. There's a shift.

I see that I am floating out of my body outside my condo building. I am definitely out of body. Everything looks normal, except for that odd glow that all physical objects have when I am out of body. I can also see only out of my right eye.

I fly way up high and watch my building get smaller and smaller. Yes, I am definitely out of body. I remember my plan, to get evidence. I decide to go to Marco and Christy's house. The instant I have this thought, I feel a strong push on my astral body and I start moving towards their apartment at about ten miles per hour.

I watch my building as I float past it. I am just about to leave it when I am shocked that I can see through the glass door directly into someone's third-story unit. I can see every detail inside their home. I am stopped instantly and propelled towards their window. I hover over their balcony and look inside. I see a man and a woman. The living room is clean and nicely furnished.

As I watch them, I become embarrassed that I am invading their privacy. This was not my plan or intention. I feel a wave of guilt and wake up. (January 1, 1996)

Most out-of-body explorers report that they have spirit guides who assist them on their journeys. Others meet advanced spiritual beings who impart sage advice.

In the majority of my own out-of-body experiences, I see nobody. I am always shocked when somebody does appear. Feeling frustrated that my own spirit guides weren't visible, I decided to try calling for them. As usual, the result was totally unexpected.

Out of Body

I lie down in bed and suddenly, I'm lucid. Feeling a bit of a shock because I was just in bed a second ago and never lost consciousness, I look around at what appears to be some type of auditorium. Closer examination reveals that I'm actually in a school cafeteria. It's very crowded. People and tables are everywhere, and there is a loud din of conversation.

As sometimes happens, my desire body takes control and I go into destructive mode. I start tipping over tables, throwing chairs. I scoop food off people's plates with my bare hands and shove it down my throat. When they get mad, I slap them in the face and push them down.

After a few moments of acting like a maniac, I fly up into the middle of the room and begin to calm down. I start thinking of various objects, and they appear instantly and magically in my hands. They look and feel totally real. I do this for a few minutes and then I remember my plan. I want to call for a highly evolved spiritual being to visit me.

I command, "I want to see a highly evolved spiritual being." To my disappointment, nothing happens. Frustrated, I fly through the roof of the cafeteria and into the sky.

I fly all over the place, doing loops, curves, dives. I keep soaring and swooping over and over, until my astral body starts zinging with energy. I am amazed and jazzed that I am still aware. I'm having so much fun that I just keep flying doing all sorts of maneuvers. I'm thinking that flying is one of the best advantages of out-of-body travel. It feels so incredibly great.

As I fly, I kind of hum happily to myself. I'm thinking of that song, "If my friends could see me now!" If only everybody knew about this, how wonderful it feels, they would change their minds about OBEs, adjust their priorities, and have as many as they could.

I fly and fly until I just can't fly anymore. It seems like I've been flying for about twenty minutes, and I can't remember ever feeling so energized.

Suddenly, there's a shift, and I'm back in my bedroom, lying in bed. My body is buzzing like the tail of an angry rattlesnake. The vibrations are fierce and roaring. I remember Monroe's technique of rolling out of body and I easily roll out of my body and fall out of bed.

I am shocked at the texture of the carpet. It feels so real. With a little effort, I manage to stand up. I can't believe I'm still out of body. I feel a wave of tiredness and fall asleep, then wake up. (January 7, 1996)

My inability to contact a higher being or spirit guide was disappointing. I had been visited several times by my mother, but as I've mentioned, in every case, she came to visit me. I never went to see her. I became extremely curious about where she was, what her life was like, and if I could visit her.

She continued to be my main inspiration for going out of body. I longed to know for sure that she was truly alive in the afterlife. And so, in many out-of-body explorations, I made it my goal to contact my mother.

In Search of My Mother

I'm running and running until I'm suddenly lucid. I feel a rush of goose bumps and am amazed to be awake. I look around me. It's daylight and I'm on a small pathway in a forest. I feel very much as though I'm out of body, and I wonder if this is a real forest. I can see everything in exquisite detail. It's a beautiful, narrow path through the woods, mostly birch, maple, and other deciduous trees. There are colorful flowers and ferns, weeds, and beautiful green shrubs and bushes.

I'm having some trouble moving. It occurs to me that I've never seen my astral body. I hold my hands out in front of me. There's a one- or two-second delay, but my hands finally come up. To my amazement, they are totally unblemished and almost translucent. Interesting.

Then I remember the main reason I am here on the astral plane. I am here to find out what happened to my mother after she died. I start calling out, "Mom! Mom! Where are you? Mother! Mom!" Over and over I call for her. My voice comes out strangely muffled, with almost no echo. I continue to call for her, and I can clearly hear my voice shouting out loudly.

To my disappointment, there is no response. I feel a wave of intense loneliness and wake up. (January 13, 1996)

Just in case anybody is wondering, it is definitely possible to feel temperature in a dream. This holds true for lucid dreams and OBEs.

I Feel Karen's Cheek

I am lucid. It is daytime and I'm in an unfamiliar location outside a building. I see a rope leading up to a high window. I climb the rope and am surprised to find my friend Karen inside. By looking at her, I can tell instantly that she is a projection and not real. She comes to the window. I lift my hand up and feel her cheek. Her flesh feels warm and soft. I say excitedly, "It is warm! It is warm!" I am totally amazed that I can feel temperature because this sensation has been conspicuously absent from nearly all my experiences. (January 27, 1996)

4

Further Astral Experiments

After doing hundreds of these types of experiments, I began to look for something new to do. Robert Monroe wrote that he was able to initiate powerful OBEs by allowing his guides or his Higher Self to take over and lead him to where he needed to go.

This seemed like a fantastic idea, particularly because the request was so open-ended. Because the astral planes are so responsive to thought, this command overcomes the problem of expectation shaping experience. Because you don't know what to expect, virtually anything can happen. I couldn't wait to try it.

Take Me Where I Need to Go

I'm lucid. I fly around my bedroom. I flap my arms to get around, but it doesn't work very well. I try to think myself upwards, but this doesn't work very well either. Frustrated, I remember what I really wanted to do. I shout out to my Higher Self, "Take me where I need to go!"

I suddenly feel my astral body sinking into the floor. The shock almost costs me my awareness, so I start spinning to maintain. It works perfectly. Overjoyed, I start singing. At first my voice cracks and sounds strange, but then it becomes clear and strong. I sing beautifully. I do several other experiments that I can't seem to recall. At one point, I am shocked to hear my bed creaking. Is my physical body moving? I am sure it's not. (February 12, 1996)

In this experience, I am certain I heard my bed creaking. At the time, I had no idea what could cause this to occur. I knew my body was paralyzed so I couldn't be moving my bed. Unless somehow my physical weight was actually fluctuating. Was such a thing even possible? I would later learn the answer.

My main problem in learning out-of-body travel was how to maintain the necessary fragile state of consciousness. Around this time, I came across a book by William Buhlman. He wrote that he was able to overcome similar difficulties by shouting the simple one-word command, "Clarity!" By now I had learned just how powerful thought can be while out of body, and I was eager to try it. To my delight, it worked beautifully and quickly became my favorite method to increase my awareness and the length of my OBEs.

Clarity!

I'm lucid. Surprise, surprise, I'm at my father's house. Another surprise, my desire body dominates my actions. I'm frustrated. I pick up books and throw them across the room. I see a pumpkin and smash it to bits. I pick up other objects— cups, pens, magazines, whatever I can lay my hands on—and I throw them. I see some people. I run up to them and run my fingers over their faces. "I'm dreaming! I'm dreaming!"

They don't seem to care. I fly through the ceiling and land in a field with cars parked around me in rows. I realize this must be a lucid dream and I feel a strong desire to project out of the illusion and into an OBE.

I feel a sudden profound heaviness. My body starts to buzz like a swarm of angry bees. I roll easily out of my body and fly straight up. I keep going up as fast as I can, until I'm suddenly high above the planet and in outer space. Looking around, I am amazed at how quickly I traveled so far out. It's dark and stars twinkle all around me. The earth lies far below me. I have never been this far out before. I totally freak out, and in a moment of panic, I whiz back down at top speed. It takes about a half-minute until I am suddenly over my condo. I fly through the roof and hover over my bed. Once I see my body under the covers, I flip over and float above it, aligning my astral body to the physical. I drift slowly down back into my physical body. I feel a thud, and suddenly I'm very heavy again and my body is buzzing like crazy.

Feeling a surge of courage, I roll out again and start flying. I decide to try flying into the "Light," as described by near-death experiencers. I'm flying around but I don't see it and don't really know where to go. I call several times for my mom, but nothing happens.

Then I feel the familiar haze coming over my thoughts. I'm about to lose consciousness when I remember Buhlman's advice to command for "clarity." I shout out, "Clarity! Clarity! Clarity!"

It works perfectly. My awareness floods into me. The scene transforms and I'm in my bedroom, floating near the corner of the ceiling in a strangely tilted position. I fall slowly back into my body and wake up, energized. (November 1, 1996)

Clarity!

I am lucid, but barely. I am clinging to my awareness like wreckage in a storm. I shout out, "Clarity! Clarity!" I feel a welcome rush of lucidity. I can think clearly, but now I have another problem. I can't see at all. Everything is pitch-black. I try to open my eyes, and boom, I wake up. (January 11, 1997)

A One-Second OBE

I feel the vibrations, roll out of body, and promptly lose consciousness. (February 21, 1997)

Occasionally, I have had OBE-type experiences that don't really fit any category, as in the following experience.

I Am Serenaded

I am lucid and getting ready to fly out of body when suddenly I hear a man and woman singing. It is very loud and melodic. These two singers are good. They have perfect pitch and incredible harmony and resonance. They sing, "It's a Small World After All." As the song progresses, they sing faster and faster, like a record on high speed. After they finish, they sing another song, which I can't quite seem to remember.

I am delighted by the performance and send out a thank you. Then I fly out of my body. I go up through the roof and hover above my condo. I fly out over the San Fernando Valley and fly over Los Angeles until I lose consciousness. (March 15, 1997)

Two days later, I had a very similar experience. Only this time, instead of singing without music, I heard a full orchestra in my head, complete with drums, brass, strings, the whole band. I felt incredibly humbled. It felt like somebody was going through an awful lot of trouble just for me.

Some of my OBEs were indistinguishable from lucid dreams. I just don't know if it involves projections or not, as in the following experience.

You Are Loved!

I'm lucid. I see G— from work, but I am sure it's not really her. I hear a lot of other banging noises and recognize them as exit noises. I walk around feeling slightly dazed. I shout out, "Clarity!" and I feel a rush of increased awareness. I see a window and I rush forward and smash the glass.

I fly through the window and sniff the ground. I can't smell anything. I start flying around. I fly through several walls and trees. I end up in a school yard. There's an 11-year-old girl walking next to her friend. I fly down and grab her shoulders. I don't think she can see me, but I feel compelled to tell her forcefully, "You are loved! You are loved!"

I am wondering just who this girl is, why I feel so compelled to talk to her and if this is all real. I wake up. (March 17, 1997)

Because of my research into the UFO phenomenon, I knew that I would probably encounter UFOs sooner or later while out of body. I never went looking for them. I don't know why, I just never felt the impulse. It happened, nevertheless, and as usual, the results were unexpected.

Out of Body, in a UFO

I'm suddenly lucid. I find myself flying quickly upwards and into a small saucer-shaped object floating in the sky above Topanga Canyon. To my amazement, I see H— on board. She is the author of a rare book on near-death experiences that I am currently reading. She is there to warn me about something, but I can't seem to remember what. I am too shocked and disoriented. (March 21, 1997)

Movement continues to be a difficult process to master while out of body. Not only is it hard to move using the power of thought, but it is also hard to keep your destination in mind long enough to get there. In fact, because your thoughts are so powerful, if you have conflicting thoughts while out of body, you will experience conflict, as in the following OBE.

OBE in the Flower Shop

I'm lucid. I can't see clearly and don't know where I am. I try to talk, but nothing comes out. I try to sing and still I can't make a sound. I peer through the haze and I can just make out a lady. I rush up her to and for some reason I ask her, "Which house?"

She replies, "2082 Burbank Boulevard," or "20082 Burbank Boulevard." I don't understand what she means, and I'm wondering what is located at this address. Suddenly, I'm at Conroy's flower shop a few blocks from my house. I have never been in the store before, though I have driven by it many times. I can't understand what I'm doing here.

I fly out the front of the store and over the street. I feel my consciousness fade so I shout out, "Clarity! Clarity! Clarity!" I feel a rush of lucidity and a surge of energy. It feels great to be out of body, so freeing and refreshing. I decide to go to Christy's house.

My astral body tugs slightly, and I'm floating at about five miles per hour towards Christy's house. This is taking a long time, and I can't seem to go any faster. Suddenly, there's another tug and I'm back at Conroy's flower shop. I wonder what I'm doing there.

Then I remember that I wanted to do an experiment. I had read earlier that some plants have elemental spirits that can be contacted while out of body. Curious, I shout out, "Show me a mint plant!" I'm flying between the rows of plants and flowers, but nothing happens. Confused, I wake up. (April 5, 1997)

As I progressed, my OBEs became longer and my experiments more complex. Finally, I was moving beyond the novice stage.

Experimenting While Out of Body

I hear a strange noise. It sounds like rushing water. It suddenly gets louder and I can feel it in my body. I pop out of body. I feel a surge of excitement. My desire body is trying to take control. I suppress the urge by sitting down and meditating. After a brief moment, I am in control enough to start experimenting.

I think of trying to read. A book manifests in my hands. I open it and start reading. I can't seem to make out the words! This isn't working.

I feel compelled to see my reflection. A mirror manifests and I look into it, but there is no reflection.

I remember that it is supposed to be difficult to control the level of light in a lucid dream. I turn on the light and the room floods with light. Looking at my bed, I think I can make out my body under the covers. Oh, my God, this isn't a dream. I'm out of body! Or am I?

With a surge of excitement, I fly down my hallway and into the next room. I am looking for proof, but I lose awareness and wake up. (April 20, 1997)

Occasionally my out-of-body adventures have landed me in uncomfortable situations. Normally, I experience no hostility from any entities or dream characters. However, it does happen, as in the following case.

Attacked by an Astral Bull

I fall out of bed and wake up (false awakening). I climb back in and fall out again, and then a third time. On the third time, I realize what is happening. I'm out of body. I fly out the window and start flying upwards as fast as I can go. There's a sudden shift.

My astral body is deposited into a small, unfamiliar field. It is daytime. Looking around, I am alarmed to see that there is a very large bull, with horns, about twenty yards away. The bull is huge, and is staring right at me, stomping and snorting.

My first instinct is to fly away. I mean, this bull is very menacing. At the same time, I fully realize that I am out of body and cannot be physically hurt. And besides, this bull is just a projection from my own mind. I certainly don't think it is a real bull.

All of this reasoning, however, doesn't change the fact that I'm about to be mauled by a bull, which doesn't sound like fun. But knowing that you are supposed to confront hostile characters, I turn around and face the bull.

It instantly charges straight at me. It covers the space between us in a split-second and hits my body with full force. It pins me tightly to the ground. I can feel the pressure of the horn. The bull is grunting and breathing heavily. I am trying to stay calm. I say softly, "Nice bull, nice bull," as if it were a cute little puppy.

The bull keeps me pinned for another second. Then it lifts its head and disappears. The scene shifts!

I am at the bottom of the driveway at my father's house,

totally out of body. I am delighted that I successfully confronted the bull, and I sing the national anthem. My voice is loud and clear.

Then I create a box of chocolate candies and I start gorging. They taste great. I wake up with energy zinging through my body. (June 16, 1997)

While my OBEs were definitely longer, the fact that I had learned how to maintain awareness didn't mean that I was able to overcome another obstacle: impatience. The following OBE is a typical example.

Experimenting While Out of Body

I'm out of body, floating in the center of my bedroom. I fly around the room a few times and then decide to do some experiments. I shout out, "Take me to a healing place!"

Suddenly, Victoria and her son, Jonathan, appear. I feel compelled to put my hands on them as if I were healing them. They disappear after I'm done. I'm left wondering what the heck just happened.

I shout out, "Take me to see my mother!" I feel a tug and I'm floating upwards. My speed increases only slightly, and I am flying for nearly a minute when I decide this is taking way too long. Knowing how short my time is out of body, I change my mind. I shout out, "Take me to see God!"

I feel another pull in a slightly different direction. I am floating along through the sky, but again, this is taking too long. I become impatient and I say, "Take me to Christy's house!"

I am pulled back downwards and I am over my condo. Then I am propelled towards Christy's house. I get about halfway there when I lose consciousness. (July 22, 1997)

Occasionally, experiences seem to defy categorization. In these experiences, the line between waking and sleeping becomes blurred to the point where the two states of consciousness exist simultaneously.

For example, around this time, I would be meditating early in the morning with my eyes closed. Suddenly, I would see my room. Thinking my eyes had somehow opened, I would sit up and realize that my eyes were actually closed.

The first few times this happened, I figured that I must have very thin eyelids, and that I was somehow able to see through them. Only later, after I read a quote from Robert Bruce, did I realize that this is actually a common experience for astral travelers. Bruce writes, "Some degree of real-time or astral sight (seeing through closed eyelids) usually manifests just before or during a successful projection exit" (Bruce, p. 307).

However, on at least two occasions, this was taken to a further extreme.

Sleeping with One Eye Open

I am lucid. I see my sister Valerie. I run up to her and tell her that she is not real and is actually my dream character. She laughs at the absurdity of my claims and obviously doesn't believe me. Her doubt causes me to have a little trouble seeing. I try opening and closing my eyes. This has often worked in the past, but this time something very strange happens.

Out of my right eye, the lucid dream scene continues. I still see Valerie and I'm in an unfamiliar room. But out of my left eye, I see my bedroom. I am lying awake in bed, looking at my room, but only out of my left eye. In my right eye, my dream is continuing. The effect is incredibly disorienting. I am both awake and asleep, lucid-dreaming and fully conscious. I am fascinated and watch for a few moments, trying to figure out what is happening. It is very disorienting. Once I realize what is happening, I am so shocked that I close and open both my eyes repeatedly. After a few moments, I am able to transfer all my consciousness back into the waking physical state. I wake up, amazed. Talk about sleeping with one eye open! I never took the saying literally, but I do now. (June 27, 1997)

While I was having successful OBEs and conducting all sorts of experiments, I still acted impulsively and with little patience.

Out-of-Body Experiments

I'm lucid. I make love to H—. It feels great. I have trouble seeing, so I open and close my eyes until my vision clears. I am in a car racing down the freeway. Knowing that it is all a mental construction, I decide to crash the car. I go spinning off the freeway and crash into the embankment. I jump out of the car and hide in the river next to the freeway.

I think of another experiment and shout out, "Mom!" She appears instantly, but I know it's not really her. It's just a projection. None of the qualities of her presence are there.

I call out, "Let me see my Higher Self!" and I promptly lose consciousness. (July 11, 1997)

Occasionally I will have lucid dreams that are clearly not OBEs and yet seem to contain levels of meaning beyond mere dreams.

The Folder

I'm lucid. I appear at Dad's house. I see Dad sleeping, so I wake him up. He looks at me and says, "I have something to show you."

He holds out his hand and shows me an object which I can't seem to remember.

I become distracted by my sisters, Victoria and Valerie. They are laughing together. I rush up to them and say, "You are dreaming! Can't you guys see, this is all a dream?"

They are not at all convinced. I fly away in disgust. The effort to convince them nearly costs me my lucidity. I feel myself falling unconscious as my vision slips away. I just barely have time to cry out, "Increase lucidity!"

It works like a charm. I am instantly totally conscious and can see with perfect clarity. I am flying through an urban area. I am going very fast. I fly right through several buildings. I am near the airport. Is this LAX? I'm not sure. I fly down and right through a jumbo jet. I keep flying until suddenly, I feel particularly attracted to a small group of people standing in a field or parking lot.

They are all well dressed and look like professionals, office-worker types. I land next to them. They approach and greet me as if they were expecting me. I have no idea who they are. I don't recognize any of them, but one man steps forward and hands me a manila folder.

I know the folder contains something very special or important, but I don't know what. I am very grateful for the gift and start thanking everyone and shaking their hands.

I reach my hand out to one man, but he will not shake it. I am sensing that he is not entirely happy with the decision to give me the folder. I feel like I understand his hesitancy and want to reassure him, but I lose my lucidity. (July 21, 1997)

My second out-of-body experiment with extraterrestrials again produced unexpected results. Because I am involved in UFO research, I have had a few sightings. And because UFO encounters can sometimes be buried in amnesia, I was eager to find out if I was able to access any memories while in another state of consciousness.

I See an Alien and Fly to the Moon

I'm lucid. I call out, "Show me my alien memories!" Perhaps not the best phrasing, but it's difficult to think while out of body. Not surprisingly, nothing happens.

I shake my head and say, "Show me any encounters I've had with aliens." Still nothing happens.

But I'm not about to give up yet. I shout out, "Okay, I want to see an alien!"

Suddenly, a figure jumps by me and runs by. I am totally shocked by its sudden appearance. It is an alien. It looks very strange, not at all like the so-called "grays" described in the UFO literature. It is about five feet tall and humanoid—meaning it has arms and legs and a head. Otherwise, it doesn't look at all human. Its legs are too long and too thin and they bend backwards. It has brownish, scaly-looking skin. Its arms are long and thin and it has clawlike fingers. Its head is strangely shaped, looking more like a dog's than a human's. It has a long snout and no hair. I am more shocked by its arrival than by its appearance. It darts quickly away.

Feeling very conscious and aware, I remember that Robert Monroe and others have made out-of-body trips to the moon. That sounded like fun, so I shout out, "Fly me to the moon!"

I am pulled sharply upwards and into the sky. After a few seconds, the bright sky becomes dark and I am surrounded by stars. Suddenly, a bright, blurry, gray shape looms in front of me. Focusing, I see it is the moon.

This is fantastic! I land down on the surface. I start looking around me. The sky is dark black and the surface of the moon is bright gray. I see rocky fields, craters and—oh, my God! There's a gigantic bubble-looking structure, like a dome-covered stadium. It is well-camouflaged and is the same color as the moon. It looks like a hill, except it's totally smooth.

I fly up and inside the structure. I am shocked to see that it is filled with all sorts of high-tech equipment. It is a very big structure with a very high ceiling. The walls are lined with display screens. There are rows of desks and tables filled with computers, wires, and all kinds of machines. I think I see a few white males in military uniform.

I fly up to one of the tables. To my shock, I see that it is a cage, and inside is a creature, a bizarre genetic experiment. It is actually a human child that has been somehow genetically altered. I can't see it clearly, and I blink my eyes and get an image of an alligator head growing out of its neck.

I'm thinking this is some unethical and bizarre genetic experiment conducted by some aspect of the U.S. military.

I am outraged and start to destroy all the equipment. I knock things over, pour water into computers, and basically trash the place. I slowly lose my lucidity and wake up. (August 2, 1997)

This experience obviously involved projection elements, and yet I feel confident that I did make it to the moon. My favorite experiment continued to be the command to my Higher Self to take control.

Take Me Where You Think I Should Go

I'm lucid. I fly around my room and then outside. I keep flying until I remember my experiments.

I call out, "Mother! Mom! Mother!" Nothing happens.

I try something else. I say, "I want to see my past lives!" Still, nothing happens.

Frustrated, I shout out, "Okay, then, take me where You think I should go."

My astral body is gripped by a huge force. Before I can even really accelerate, there's a shift and I'm standing in another place. It is a beautiful rain forest. It looks like Olympia National Forest in Washington. There are tall Sequoia trees covered with moss, lots of ferns, and other plants. Dappled sunlight is coming down through the canopy of trees. The life force of this place is incredible.

I walk through the forest, soaking up the nature energies. I don't know where I am, but this place is great. As I walk, I come upon a clearing. Inside the clearing is a clear, cool river. At the far end of the clearing is a tall waterfall. The water is pure blue and white. The green on the trees is incredibly vivid. Everything is so stunningly beautiful.

I walk into the river. The water reaches up to my thighs and swirls around me just like normal water. I am amazed by its texture and the fact that it doesn't get me wet. It has a subtle coolness.

I am playing with the water when I suddenly see someone standing near me. It is Lucas, someone I used to baby-sit. I am amazed, and think, "Why do I need to see him?" He smiles at me and we splash together in the water. I wake up energized and in a great mood. (August 17, 1997)

Even at this late stage, I continued to have problems differentiating lucid dreams from OBEs.

No Illusions!

I'm lucid. I pop out and appear at Dad's house. I'm wondering, is this real or is this illusory? I spin around and look around me. I'm still at Dad's house. I guess this is an OBE. Just to make sure, I shout out, "No illusions!" Absolutely nothing changes. Everything looks just like it does in normal physical life. I fly up into the middle of the room and head out the window. Bam! I splat against the window, bouncing off it and landing on the floor. I am so astonished I lose consciousness. (December 6, 1997)

OBE Turns into Lucid Dream

I am out of body. I am very excited. I start flying through the walls of my condo, spinning and doing loops. I keep flying and doing maneuvers until I'm suddenly pulled back into my body. Suddenly I am lying back in bed, still totally lucid. Instead of going out of body, I practice visualizations. I visualize a car and it appears in perfect clarity. I visualize a pathway in a forest and instantly, I'm walking along the path. It looks totally realistic and is far more detailed than I originally imagined it. I walk down the pathway until I can't remember. (December 21, 1997)

According to researcher and lucid dreamer Alan Worsley, creating a television and manipulating the controls is an excellent way to learn control of the lucid state. He writes of his own attempts, "I have experimented with manipulating imagery, as if I were learning to operate by trial an internal computer video system (including 'scrolling,' 'panning,' changing the scene instantly, and 'zooming.') Further, I have experimented with isolating part of the imagery or 'parking' it, by surrounding it with a frame such as a picture frame or proscenium arch and backing away from it" (LaBerge 1990, p. 128).

My own experiments with dream televisions were not quite as controlled, but still a lot of fun.

Astral Television

I wake up (false awakening). Marco and Christy are sleeping together in a bunk bed. I'm shouting Marco's name, but he can't hear me. He's complaining to Christy about a toothache. I say, "Christy?" She tilts her head and sits up. I repeat, "Christy! Christy!" I can barely speak and suddenly realize this is a dream. I am lucid. I fly up out of the bedroom and go into the living room.

I see the television and I remember the experiment. I flick the knob and it hums to life. I try to adjust the volume, but nothing happens. I switch channels and different scenes appear on the screen, but I can't seem to remember what they are.

Suddenly my brother Jamey is there, and he is harassing me. I see Diane, and Jamey starts harassing her. I start to move away but I remember that you're supposed to confront hostile dream characters. So I ask Jamey, "What are you doing?"

"Nothing," he says, childishly.

"Stop it!" I say.

Jamey just looks at me dumbly and keeps poking at Diane. I step between Jamey and Diane and I try reasoning with him. I tell him, "You don't want to hurt Diane. She's a nice lady."

Jamey doesn't reply, but reaches past me to hit Diane in the head.

I shout out, "No!" pulling Diane away. Jamey promptly evaporates.

Suddenly the whole scene flickers and starts to fade. I float up and spin a couple of times. The house appears back in perfect clarity. I try to fly out the window, but bounce off. After a few tries, I make it outside.

Standing in the driveway, I see a fountain of water in the corner of the garage. I suddenly realize my mouth is very dry and I bend over to get a drink. I can just barely taste and feel the water and my thirst is insatiable.

There's somebody behind me. It's my nephew and niece. I walk up to them and tell them, "Look, I can fly!"

I soar upwards about fifteen feet, do a couple of whirls, and look back. They're looking at me in amazement. I lose awareness and wake up. (August 7, 2000)

Throughout this time, I was having numerous psychic experiences, mostly involving precognition. The following OBE/lucid dream gave me a clue as to why.

My Third Eye

I'm suddenly lucid. I start flying through my condo, carefully examining my surroundings. I almost lose awareness, but spinning brings me back. I remain aware, but a great deal happens here that I am unable to recall.

Later, I see somebody and have sex. With my desire body satiated, I call out, "Mom! Mom! Mom!" As usual, nothing happens.

Frustrated, I shout out, "Clarity! Clarity! Clarity!" My awareness sharpens. As sometimes happens, I find myself looking in a mirror. My vision is blurry at first but slowly gets back to normal. I am shocked by my reflection in the mirror. My eyes are dark and small and Asian-looking. As I examine them, this effect becomes more exaggerated. Suddenly, there's something appearing on my forehead. A third eye appears in the center of my forehead! It opens and winks at me. (August 12, 2000)

More TV and Reading Experiments

I'm lucid. I slide out of my body feet-first and stand up. I remember I want to try reading. I see a clock and peer at its face. First, only the numbers on the left side are visible. Then they disappear and I can see only the numbers on the right side. Then all the numbers appear, but they are spinning like a merry-go-round. I laugh at the futility of the experiment and decide to try something else.

I create a television and turn it on. The screen comes to life. An old Western movie is playing. I adjust the volume knob, but I can't seem to control the level of sound. I switch channels to a game show, then to a situation comedy. I don't recognize any of the programs. (December 20, 2000)

Most advanced projectors have been able to get proof that

their experiences are real. Even though I was certain I was having OBEs, I had never gotten proof good enough to satisfy me. I began to focus on finding a location that I could visit later in the physical and confirm details.

Out of Body, Singing

I'm lying in bed. I feel the rushing vibrations. They get stronger until suddenly I whiz out of my body. I slowly open one eye and then the other. I can just barely see. I fly around. I try several times to see my bed or my room, but my vision fades each time I try to focus. Each time I just manage to get my vision back.

I try to fly through a window, but bounce off it. It takes me three or four tries to get through. Once I do, I am certain I am out of body. I am floating three stories up outside my condo. I remember my desire to fly under the bridge near my house. I see it and fly underneath it. I am so happy to have been able to exercise such control that I start singing in celebration. Suddenly, I hear another voice singing along with me. Somebody is with me! Is this my spirit guide? I just don't seem to be able to generate enough awareness to continue the experience, and I fall asleep. (March 10, 2001)

Proof!

I'm lying in bed when I feel the vibrations. It feels like my body is a hollow tube and there's water rushing through it. But I can still feel my body. I'm too physical. I feel a split-second lapse of consciousness and suddenly I'm out of body. I start running around and flying. A television appears in front of me. It's already on. There's a program on, showing a snowy scene. I change the channel. The screen fades to black, then brightens to a featureless screen. I turn up the sound. I change the channel a couple of times and a different scene comes on. A beach scene? A war scene? I repeat the scenes to myself, but I can't seem to recall them.

There's a shift, and I'm back in my body feeling the vibrations. I remember the "Flash" technique [described later] of going out of body. I start running and I run straight out of my body. I keep going until, like a rubber-band, I am snapped back into my body.

I feel the rushing feelings. I'm frustrated that I can't seem to stay out of body, but then I remember Robert Bruce's advice that a series of short, consecutive, remembered OBEs is better than one long, half-remembered one. I use the roll-out technique. I roll out, and land standing up. I am totally out of body with a clear, crisp consciousness. Looking around me, I see my room in perfect clarity. I fly out the window and hover at the edge of my condo. It's early morning and everything is so beautiful.

It feels great to be out of body and in control. I decide to fly under the bridge near my house. As I fly under the bridge, I notice something bizarre. The L.A. River is a cement river with cement sides. However, as I look at the bank of the river, I see it is filled with earth. There is at least two feet of soil along the edge, and it is thick with grass and small weeds. Small pieces of litter dot the soil. I see paper, cartons, and a few cans.

I study the scene carefully because I am certain that there is no soil in the river. It's cemented! I am thinking this part must be a projection because there are no dirt banks. Still, I am jazzed to be out of body and I am soaking up the soothing energies. (March 22, 2001)

The next day, I went to the bridge to see if there really were dirt banks. To my shock, a dirt bank about two feet thick covered the cement river bank under the bridge, exactly where I had seen it. I was totally delighted to see this. Even though I noticed what I thought were a few slight variations in what I remembered, the resemblance was undeniable. But what made it so pivotal for me was that I was able to confirm the scene to a degree that proved to me that I was actually going out of body. It was particularly convincing because I could not have predicted it. I would never have thought that such a huge volume of soil could collect there, and yet it did.

I continued to experiment using the TV and also radio experiments. I highly recommend that projectors try this as the results are always interesting.

Do You Believe?

I'm lying in bed awake and relaxed when I suddenly feel the sensation of bodily heaviness. I go with the feeling and relax. My body gets increasingly heavy. It feels like I'm being physically pressed down into my mattress. Suddenly, I lose all physical sensation and I start spinning in pure blackness. I slowly open my eyes and see a small spot of light which slowly expands around me. I'm out of body, in my bedroom. I see Valerie.

I fly out the window, and pop! I'm in the back bedroom at Dad's house. I see a radio and realize that it is there so I can perform control experiments.

I turn on the radio and it starts whining like an old-fashioned radio set. I tune the stations. Suddenly, the reception is clear and I hear Jim Croce singing, "Moving on Down the Highway." It sounds exactly as it does in real life. I'm wondering if there's a message there for me. Am I moving down the highway of spiritual evolution?

I change the station. I hear Cher singing, "Do You Believe in Life after Love?" I am amazed by the realistic quality of the music and delighted by the obvious message.

I change the station again, wondering what song will appear. It's Steve Miller singing, "Fly Like an Eagle." I feel so grateful that I'm overcome with emotion and lose consciousness. (September 15, 2001)

By this time, I was able to maintain consciousness long enough to conduct experiments pretty much every time I got out. I began to experiment with different methods of going out of body. One popular method that I had never tried was climbing out of my body using an imaginary rope. Sounded like fun.

The Rope Technique

I feel the vibrations and now I'm ready to go out. I decide to use the rope technique. I visualize a rope hanging down from the ceiling above my bed. I can't see it, but reaching out with my astral arms, I can definitely feel it. I am surprised because my rope feels more like a hard pole. "Whatever works," I think, and I start climbing hand over hand up the pole. It's a strange sensation to pull myself out. I usually get out of my body quickly. This time, I slowly pull myself out. It feels kind of like pulling dry glue off your skin. There's a slight tension or suction, but I easily pop out. The pole disappears and I float to a walking position. I'm bobbing around my bedroom.

I decide to try to see my body. I have rarely been able to do this, and never to the level where I could clearly see my face. I'm looking at my bed, but there's nobody in it! I run my hands across the surface, searching for my body. I can't find it, so I lift the blankets and push them off. The bed is empty, and it occurs to me that if I'm moving blankets, then this is at least partially illusory.

All of a sudden, I hear a loud squeal, as if somebody stepped on a pig. I'm thinking this is either an astral distraction or astral wildlife and I ignore it. I keep walking around my room, testing reality, trying to determine if this is a projection or my actual room.

There's a shift and I'm with my friend Roger. I'm explaining to him the special properties of the astral plane, that you simply have to think a thought and it will instantly manifest. I'm showing him how to do it. I demonstrate for him, creating first objects and then people. Roger seems a little dopey and out of it. I don't think he's getting it.

I look around us. We are in a wide underground cement tunnel. It looks like a subway, except wider. We walk down the tunnel as I continue explaining things to Roger.

There's a man on a bench looking at us. As usual, I am shocked to see somebody. I don't know who he is, and I certainly didn't manifest him, at least not consciously.

I walk up to him and for some bizarre reason I ask him, "Who is Einstein?"

He rolls his eyes and says, "You are!" as if it were obvious.

I know good and well I'm not Einstein and am confused by his answer. Then I ask him, again I don't know why, "Well then, who is Thomas Edison?"

He turns to Roger and says, "You are!"

I don't understand him. He's got to be confused or kidding. I shake my head and fly away. I keep flying for several minutes, just playing, doing loops, dives and curls, and practicing my astral vision. (June 15, 2002)

Occasionally during a projection, I have become aware not only of my out-of-body environment, but of my physical environment. In other words, even while I'm out there exploring the astral planes, I can sometimes still feel my body. I can hear traffic noises, and in a couple of cases, I got clear visual impressions of my bedroom.

This was very confusing to me at first, especially because there was no mention of this in the OBE literature. It wasn't until I read the works of Bruce Moen and Robert Bruce that I realized I wasn't alone. Both Moen and Bruce have reported having OBEs while still remaining conscious in the physical body. I had already had a similar experience with sleeping with one eye open and several OBEs involving dual perception. However, this next experience made me realize that it is possible to have an OBE while still remaining conscious of the physical body. I was very excited about this latest development. It felt very much like the beginnings of bilocation.

Bilocation

I feel the vibrations. I pop in and out of my body several times; this seems to help my control. I have excellent vision and motion. I am also in control of my thoughts and emotions. I fly straight up at rocket speed and pop into the astral dimension. I am at the place where I can create imagery with perfect ease. I start creating all kinds of objects and scenes. I am very pleased, but realize that I've done this a thousand times. I need something more challenging.

Lately, I've been working with sound. I think of the song, "Black Magic Woman." Although I don't consciously know the song that well, it plays in perfect clarity. The sound is all around me. Best stereo sound I've ever heard.

I have some trouble controlling my amazement so I start flying around and around. I feel my memory slip and I realize I'm losing track of what's happening. I can see what's happening, but I am forgetting each moment as it passes.

I slow down and center myself. I hold on to my awareness and commit what I've seen so far to memory. I stay this way for a few moments, sort of meditating and not allowing anything to distract me. I'm trying to gain full access to my memory and awareness.

Suddenly, something strange happens. I feel my awareness level expanding, splitting or changing somehow. I can feel my physical body! I can feel exactly what position it's in. In fact, I can feel myself inside it, and I can sense my bedroom around me. At the same time, I'm still out of body, and it feels like I'm far, far away in another dimension.

This is fascinating. I don't even have to shift my awareness back and forth. I'm equally aware of both locations at one time.

I have experienced this before, but never so strong, and I'm very impressed. I explore the perceptions of my physical body. I realize that I could stand up and walk around. I am very, very close to waking consciousness while still remaining totally out of body. I remain this way for about thirty seconds before waking up. (July 22, 2002)

Probably about one in five of my projections involves a sensation of bodily heaviness. According to the literature, this is just one of many physical "exit" sensations that projectors experience. I have experienced pretty much every sensation in the books, including lightness, heaviness, vertigo, eroticism, vibrations, buzzing, choking, thirst, hunger, temperature variations, and others.

As far as I have been able to determine, however, the physical body itself manifests none of these symptoms. In other words, although the vibrations may have felt so strong I was convinced I was flopping around on the bed, further experiments proved I was not.

However, according to several reports, amazing physical effects are possible, including levitation or increased weight. These, like astral travel, are one of the many siddhis or psychic powers as described by Patanjali, the founder of the Yoga Sutras. I was particularly interested in these effects, especially after the following experience.

Increasing Weight

I lie face down on my couch, one arm hanging down to the floor. After about fifteen minutes I am very relaxed and feel the paralysis creep over my body. Then my body starts to feel very heavy. To my astonishment, I hear the leather couch creak heavily underneath me. It is a loud couch and responds audibly to movement. The only thing is, my body is totally paralyzed. I am absolutely certain I am not moving my arms or legs. The only movement I feel is increased weight. I feel my head sink down last. I am so amazed that I lose the vibrations. (August 2, 2002)

I can only wonder if my weight is really increasing. It sure feels like it, but there's very little literature on this that I can find. Levitation is a subject I've investigated for years, but accounts of increased weight were almost unheard of. I was able to find cases of increased weight in cases of demonic possession, but I was pretty sure I wasn't possessed. Then I heard about a little girl who possessed the so-called "Odic" force. As she demonstrated on television, she claimed to be able to increase her weight. She appeared to go into a trance, and then a weight lifter attempted to lift her up. He appeared to be unable to do so. This is one area that I plan to explore in the future. My idea is to sleep on a bed on a scale, induce the heaviness and see if my weight actually changes.

Meanwhile, I was still obsessed with seeing my body or getting some kind of proof that I was going out of body.

I Look for David

It's early morning and I'm lying in bed. I roll over and relax. After a few seconds, I feel the vibrations. I let go of my body and start twirling uncontrollably. After a few seconds, I pop out, but I can't see. With a few moments of concentration, I'm able to clear my vision. I hold up my hands and they appear, unblemished and ethereal, but otherwise normal. I start looking around me, but all I see are scattered objects. I'm having trouble perceiving if I'm in my room or just projecting thoughts. I see my bed. I feel across it foot by foot, finally stripping off the blankets, but I cannot find my body. It is not there. Or am I trapped in a lucid dream?

Knowing that this is wasting time, I abandon it for better pursuits. I want to find David. I call out for him and suddenly I am flying. As I fly, my vision and awareness slowly increase. I see that I am over the ocean and I remember that David is in Mexico. I fly for about a minute, until I lose consciousness. (August 5, 2002)

Being unable to maintain control is one of the many obstacles to being able to travel out of body. Control comes in many forms. Controlling emotion, controlling movement, controlling manifestations. If you think controlling yourself in the waking state is hard, try doing it while out of body.

Control of the dream state is one of the methods used by Buddhists to reach spiritual enlightenment. If one can control the dream state, the same abilities will eventually translate into the waking state.

Control

Lucid. Looking around, I'm in a grocery store in the produce section. People around me are shopping. Normally, my desire body takes control and goes crazy, eating everything in sight, breaking anything it can find, and then manifesting sexy people to have sex. This time, I maintain control. I walk carefully through the store observing.

I am having some recall problems. I start changing things into opposites. I think I see a lot of something, and make it few. I see something big and make it small, I think. What I really remember is seeing a man with a red shirt. I turn it blue.

I rush up to the front of the store. People are waiting in lines to check out their items. I cut to the front of one of the lines. I grab the intercom and make a storewide announcement. I say, "Can anyone here go lucid? Would all lucid people please report to the front!" Unfortunately I am unable to complete my request as the power to the intercom suddenly cuts off! I wake up. (August 14, 2002)

Robert Bruce writes that the astral body is actually a mental projection and that the true form of the astral body is a small point of consciousness. I have experienced this, and yet, in many of my projections I have seen my hands and feet. Bruce writes that a prolonged stare at one's hands will reveal the true nature of the astral body, and that one's hands will actually melt or disappear.

I had seen my astral body many times, especially my hands, but they had never melted. But then again, I never stared at them for a long time.

I Examine My Astral Hands

I pop out of my body. I instantly remember my intention to look at my hands and see if Robert Bruce is correct. I lift up my hands in front of me. I see them! They look unusually young and unblemished, but otherwise normal. I remember to keep looking. I turn them over and over. Suddenly, I see them begin to melt. The effect is startling and very strange. I watch carefully as each of my fingers melts and fades away. Then my hands disappear and I have nothing but two stumps on the end of my arms. Then my arms start to melt. This is very strange. Robert

Bruce is right. The astral body does melt. I am so amazed, I wake up. (September 2, 2002)

While most of my later projections involve few or no exit sensations or exit distractions, I do occasionally experience them. Sometimes it can get pretty intense. Writes Robert Bruce, "The feelings that can be generated by heavy exit sensations, if not fully prepared for, can cause needless terror and panic. . . . In the majority of cases, projectors were forced to abort their first successful exit simply because they were unprepared for the enormity of the resulting sensations. Please do not think I am exaggerating here. This is a major issue for all new projectors! . . . Astral noises may be heard during the exit, with scary voices and things going bump in the night, like chains dragging, sinister giggling and muttering, evil laughter, and nasty growling and snarling. . . . Astral noises are quite common during the exit, but always cease the moment the exit is complete. It is much more common for new projectors to hear astral noises and voices than for more seasoned projectors. . . . Any and all astral noises must be totally ignored during the exit stage of an OBE. . . . you may feel cold and clammy hands, grabbing and clutching at your body. You may even see faces leering and snarling at you" (Bruce, pp. 496, 510).

Exit Distractions

It's the middle of the day, but everything is very peaceful and quiet, so I decide to try to have an OBE. I lie down in bed and begin to relax. In about five minutes, I am relaxed enough. I feel the vibrations and increase them. I feel a sense of vertigo and dizziness. My body is rushing and vibrating intensely but I can't seem to pop out. Suddenly, I hear a lot of exit noises. I hear what sounds like heavy furniture being moved around. I hear the voices of several people talking at once. Then I hear the sound of a large jet or a waterfall. This is intense! I hear more voices.

I'm feeling a strong surge of energy and I am about to lift out when suddenly I hear my nephew's voice cry out urgently, "Take me with you!" I am so surprised by this request that I snap back to waking awareness. (September 6, 2002)

All of the above experiences taught me just how powerful thought is on the astral planes. However, after doing so many experiments, I decided it was time to do some real explorations.

5

People and Animals
on the Astral Plane

While the majority of my OBEs involve no other people, this is not always the case. I have been able to visit many people. Sometimes they are dead. Sometimes they are living. I also continued to have uncontrolled (by me at least) OBEs in which I would visit my mother. These visits actually started before I learned how to go out of body, and occurred on a fairly regular basis.

I See Mom
I wake up and I see Mom's face hovering next to my bed. She moves around the bed, looking at me. I laugh because at times her face gets so low to the ground that her body wouldn't have fit. She is smiling and looking at me. I feel very strongly that it is truly her. I feel her presence, and waves of love coming from her. She seems pleased that I am convinced it is really she. She knows that I will remember this meeting and is happy about it. So am I! As usual, she never utters a word. (May 21, 1989)

My mother's death sent me on this adventure. And my desire to know what happened to her was my main inspiration to go out of body. I knew that one day I would find out what life is like for her on the astral plane.

Looking back, I can see that I was being pretty selfish. I now know that she visits me on a nightly basis. Again, the trick is remembering. Although I have had normal dreams about my mother, there is always a certain quality to visitations that convinces me that I am dealing with a real person.

I See Mom!

I walk into the living room, and I am shocked to see my mother sitting at the dining room table. I know that she is dead, and can't believe she is really there. Now that I see her, I remember that we visit constantly. I can't believe I had forgotten this, but she seems to understand my situation. I am so happy to see her that it takes all my effort to control my emotion. I know that I usually rush up to her and hug her uncontrollably. This time I manage to walk up to her slowly, showing her that I have finally managed to control myself.

She looks at me and smiles warmly. I reach out to hug her and she completely surprises me by reaching out, lifting me up by my armpits and swinging me around. I laugh in delight. This was something she could never have done unless we were both out of body, as she would never have been able to lift me like that. I am very happy to see her again, and vow to remember that she is not really dead, and that I see her all the time. (November 27, 1990)

In the preceding experience, I remembered seeing my mother practically every night. Whenever my mother visited me, I would remember all the other times we had been together in the dream state, although I can't remember them consciously. I can only remember *remembering* them.

I began to remember more and more visits from my mother.

Usually, these occurred in the early hours of the morning, when I was most deeply asleep. Because these visits were therefore especially hard to remember, and I usually only brought back snippets. I wonder if this is why so many people don't believe in life after death. For some reason, it is extremely difficult to bring back memories from this particular state of consciousness where the dead can interact with the living.

Still, I am becoming increasingly convinced that it happens nightly.

I Meet Mom

I wake up and am shocked to see that I'm with Mom. Overcome with emotion, I kneel down and kiss her hand. I'm too excited to stay conscious. (February 12, 1992)

I Meet Mom

I'm sitting on the couch next to Mom. I know she's dead, and she knows I'm alive. She knows that I'm struggling to remember our visits, and she seems to be sympathetic to my plight. We talk about a lot of subjects, life, love, sex, and everything in between. (March 17, 1992)

Upon awakening, I was amazed by the peculiar quality of memory in the dream state. In the last dream, I distinctly remembered long conversations. However, upon awakening, I couldn't remember a single exchange.

Again, I remembered remembering, but I couldn't actually remember. I know that doesn't make much sense, but neither does being asleep and awake at the same time.

I have not only had visits from deceased people, but from animals also, specifically our late dog Maxine.

Maxine Visits Me

Maxine comes to visit me. She comes up and licks me, which is something she did only rarely when she was very glad to see me. She was a graceful, beautiful, strong, loyal dog. Her presence is very joyful and realistic. I feel like I am actually in her presence. I am convinced this is my dog. (April 18, 1992)

Maxine Visits Me Again!

As if to make a point, Maxine visits me again. I'm in an environment with no features whatsoever. Maybe gray fog, but nothing to see. This is the place where I usually meet my mother. Suddenly, I see Maxine. She walks up to me and licks my face as I pet her. I am amazed, lucid, and very happy to see her. (April 22, 1992)

I Visit Maxine

I am in a dark place with no features when suddenly I see Maxine. She looks totally real and is radiating love. I am convinced it is really her. (July 19, 1992)

One of the best advantages of going out of body is the ability to visit deceased loved ones. The feelings of reunion are always intense. It's a transformational experience and really convinces you about the reality of life after death.

I Visit Mom

Suddenly, I wake up and realize that I'm sitting next to my mother. I am so delighted and happy. I sit next to her and soak up her presence. Again, I can't believe that I ever thought she was dead. I remember visiting her hundreds and hundreds of times. As we sit and talk, I vow that I will never, ever believe again that she's dead. (August 1, 1992)

After waking up from these OBEs, I always have a feeling of culture shock. When I'm out of body, it's like being in a different world, and the physical world seems so far away. I feel like it is the real world, and the physical world is the dreamworld. Waking up and finding myself with a physical body is something I continually have to get used to.

Of course, the same thing goes every time I get out of body.

My dog Maxine regularly came to visit me. Interestingly, she always came twice in a row, usually a few days apart.

Maxine

I'm in a gray, featureless place when Maxine rushes up to me. I embrace her. (October 22, 1995)

Maxine

I see Maxine. She runs up to me. I find potato skins and I try to feed them to her. She doesn't care about them. She is happy to see me. She licks me in a very loving way. I am convinced it is her. (October 29, 1995)

I continued to visit my mom on a fairly regular basis.

I Visit Mom

I'm lucid. Mom appears in front of me. Overcome with emotion, I run over and sit down at her feet. I feel incredibly humbled by her love. I have so many questions that I want to ask; they are tumbling all over each other in my head. I am unable to maintain my awareness and fall asleep. (April 23, 1996)

I Visit Mom

I see Mom and am propelled into lucidity. I'm unusually self-composed, and take the opportunity to tell her I love her and really enjoy being in her presence. We are able to talk and walk for a long time, though I can't remember the conversation. I am just so amazed that I ever thought she was dead. She's alive and as well as can be. Now that I'm with her, I remember hundreds of similar visits. I know I will forget them when I go back to the physical world and am trying very hard to remember everything that occurs. I feel like I'm living in two worlds, one where my mom is living and another where she is not. (September 17, 1996)

I See Mom

I see Mom. She doesn't speak, but sits properly with a slight, knowing smile. I stare at her as I try to deal with the flood of memories. I can't believe I ever forgot this! I am amazingly aware this time and am able to walk around Mom and examine her from all sides. She calmly and politely poses for me. I touch her shoulders and face, and talk to her. It feels great to be in her presence again. I see Victoria there. She doesn't think that anything unusual is happening. (August 4, 2000)

I See Mom

I meet Mom. She is sitting on the couch and the whole family is there. We are all talking and having a good time. I'm struggling to remain lucid. I can't believe this is happening. (September 2, 2000)

I still continued to have regular visits with my mom. On February 24, 2001, on March 2, 2001, on August 5, 2002—each time it's the same. I'm totally shocked as memories flood into my brain—memories that I can access there, but not after I wake up.

Occasionally, when out of body, I would see other living family members who were also out of body, though they didn't realize it.

I See Dad!

I wake up because someone is in my room. I look and see that Dad is standing next to my bed. I think, how strange that he would come into my room in the middle of the night and just stand there. I suddenly realize why this seems so strange. I must be dreaming. But I am totally awake. I am a little confused because usually this is how Mom appears to me, and she's dead. I am fully aware that Dad is alive. Oh, my God! It suddenly occurs to me that Dad is out of his body too. I jump up to tell him, and he slowly dematerializes and fades away. (August 10, 1989)

That morning, I told Dad that I dreamed he came into my room. He laughed and said, "That's funny. Last night I dreamed that I had wings and was flying all over the house."

I told him that he was out of body and he woke me up. I knew he didn't believe me, but I just couldn't resist. As most OBEers will tell you, flying dreams are almost always half-remembered OBEs.

Visitations with real-life people continued.

I See Christy

I'm lucid. I'm in the place with no features, just a grayish, glowing fog. Suddenly, I see Christy's face in front of me. She is smiling widely and is obviously happy to see me. I am happy to see her, and amazed because I know she is alive, not dead. I can tell instantly that this is really her and not a projection. Projections act woodenly and have no spark of consciousness in their eyes. Real people exude love and self-awareness and the quality of their personality is readily apparent. I know this is really Christy. I am so happy to see her.

I react like I usually do when I see a real person while out of body. I reach out to touch her. I hold Christy's face with both hands and caress her cheeks. We are both smiling and very happy to meet each other out of body. (June 5, 1994)

I immediately called Christy to see if she recalled any unusual experiences that evening. She denied any memory of meeting me. I was disappointed, and vowed that someday we would meet out of body. Shortly later, we finally achieved a measure of success in this area.

OBE

I'm lucid. I get overly excited and fly out the window and lose consciousness. (November 20, 1994)

Although I have no recall of what happened, Christy says that on this day, she had a lucid dream and I was in it. We also had several mutual dreams, in which we both remembered experiencing the same events. Although these were only dreams, many dreams are actually memories of out-of-body experiences.

One of my most profound OBE visitations also provided some interesting validation that my OBEs were real.

I See Rex Out of Body

I'm out of body. I shout out, "Take me to see Mom!" I am propelled upwards through the ceiling. There's a pronounced shift and I'm in another dimension. It's very foggy around me. I recognize this place. This is where I meet Maxine or my mother. Suddenly I see Rex. I am amazed because he's alive.

I rush forward and grab his shoulders. "Rex, what are you doing here?"

He just smiles and looks at me with a slightly bewildered expression. He looks great. Normally, in real life, he has health problems and he's a little hunched over. However, here I can't believe how healthy he looks. He's literally glowing. I am laughing because even though he's a black man, he has white light coming off him. I am shocked to see him there and looking so good that I just hug him. (June 11, 1995)

Rex is a family friend and I was shocked to see him. I, of course, planned to call him up and ask him if he remembered any strange "dreams" lately. That's when I got the news that he had just had a severe stroke.

Another strange experience that seemed to involve real people occurred a few years later.

I Fly To Mary's House

I am lucid, floating in the middle of my room above my bed. I shout out, "Take me to the *Titanic!*" Nothing happens.

I look around my room. Although it looks real, I am determined to make sure that I am actually out of body and not lucid-dreaming. I shout out, "All illusion disappear!" Nothing happens.

All right then, I am out of body. I have a sudden urge to fly over to Mary's house in San Francisco. As soon as I have the thought, there's a shift, and I am there. I am amazed, as the distance is a few hundred miles.

There is no sense of travel whatsoever. I am standing on the sidewalk in front of Mary's house. I see two children, about eight and eleven years old. I have no idea who they are but I feel compelled to approach them.

They look at me expectantly. I tell them, "Did you know that you're out of your bodies?"

They don't seem to understand. I try again. "Would you like to fly?"

They agree enthusiastically. I take each of them by the hand and we fly off together. (September 13, 1997)

A similar experience occurred with my niece.

I Fly with Mudita

I am lucid, but can't seem to see. I use the spinning technique to increase my awareness. After a few spins, I stop and look around. I am in my bedroom, definitely out of body.

I shout out, "Take me to Christy's!"

I am pulled up out of my bedroom and over the San Fernando Valley towards Christy's house. Although it's a clear, sunny morning, I fly through little bits of mist and clouds on the way. Suddenly, I'm over her apartment and I plop down through the roof, feet first, and land in the living room. I look around for something I can use as proof.

Suddenly, I see Mudita. She is smiling and looking great. I know it is really her because all the qualities of her actual presence are there. She seems to understand my intention to find Christy and she leads me into Christy's bedroom. She's not there, so we take each other's hands and fly off into the sky together. It is great fun. (September 21, 1997)

I Visit Marco

I am lucid. Looking around, I see I am at my father's house. Man, this is frustrating. Why do I always start here? I wonder if this is a lucid dream or if I am out of body. I spin several times to erase illusion. Looking around me, I am still at Dad's house. Seems real enough to me.

I fly around the living room a few times, then through the back sliding glass door and out into the backyard. I fly several hundred feet above the house and then swoop down. Everything looks real.

I see a van driving down Cheney Drive. I am instantly drawn to it like a magnet. I follow it as it heads down the road. I can't quite keep up with it. By this time, I am right next to a neighbor's house. I think about entering it, but knowing it would be a violation of privacy, I decide not to do it.

Suddenly, Marco appears. He looks at me and smiles in his sparkly way. I can tell instantly that it's really him and not a projection. I rush up to him and hold his face in my hands. Although I see him all the time in real life, I am incredibly happy to see him. I hold his face and soak up his presence. I am amazed because I can feel his cheeks as if they were physical. But I know they're not. (September 27, 1997)

Most of my family members do not recall these visits. Only Christy has been able to recall one meeting. However, this appears to be normal. Most people are unable to recall their dreams, much less their OBEs. They are what Marilyn Hughes calls "subconscious astral."

Many times I have found my extended family visiting each other on the astral plane. As we are all sitting at a table, my mother is looking at me. She knows that I am lucid and that I will remember these meetings, while everyone else in the room thinks they are already awake, or they know that they are not at the point where they are able to remember. How somebody can know that they won't remember is beyond me. However, when I'm there, I know I *will* remember.

I Will Remember

I pop out of my body. I try really hard to see my body in bed but I just can't seem to do it. I fly outside. Again, I have a hard time getting through my bedroom window.

I pop through and I'm in another place. Suddenly, I see Valerie and Victoria. They are real. I float in front of Victoria and look her directly in the eye. She avoids my gaze. She hesitates and resists, but finally looks at me.

Then I see Mom. I am shocked as a flood of memories pour into me. Everyone else around seems to think that this is the only life we live, that we are all awake and that Mom has always been alive. But I know that she's dead. Everyone else around is subconscious astral, and I am struggling to sort it all out. But as usual, I am too excited to see Mom. However, I am enough in control to calmly ask her to hug me.

I am trying to get Victoria to remember this meeting. What will make her remember? My mind creates a UFO. Victoria and I witness this awesome UFO sighting together. I see I have her attention. I tell her that now she will remember. She says, "Yeah, but I'm in that weird in-between state." She seems to have some awareness of physical life.

I say, "Oh, my God! I am too. But I will remember. And so will you!"

She looks at me doubtfully.

I tell her over and over again, "Remember the UFO!" (September 9, 2001)

Unfortunately, Victoria had no dream memory of any UFO sighting or any dreams. On another occasion, I met my brother Steven and tried to get him to remember.

I Visit Steven

I'm lucid. I look around me. I'm at Dad's house. I rip open a window and fly through. I see Steven! I know it's him. I rush up to him and ask, "Will you remember this?"

He says firmly, "No!"

I am upset and begin to argue with him. I say, "You will remember. You must remember! Why can't you remember? Remember!"

He gets mad and says, "I won't remember!"

I look at him in frustration and say, "Well, I will." (October 10, 2001)

Needless to say, Steven didn't remember. I have seen a few other people on the astral plane, including my spirit guides. The most interesting of these are presented in a later chapter.

One of my most recent visitations occurred a few weeks following the death of a family dog, Rouster. After he died, I was certain that I would be able to locate his spirit, as I had a strong connection with him. I was not surprised when I found him, but I was surprised at what happened when I did.

I Meet Rouster

I'm jolted into lucidity by the appearance of Rouster running up to me. He's very excited to see me, wagging his tail and jumping up. I amazed because he's just like a little puppy. He looks so young. He bites my hand. I laugh because as a puppy, Rouster had a problem with biting things. Seems like things are back to normal. Suddenly, my other dogs, Maxine and Clyde, are there too. They jump up and demand equal time. I pet them all. It feels great to be with them. (March 23, 2003)

I've since met Rouster on three other occasions. He seems to be doing quite well.

6

Food and Sex on the Astral Plane

One of the first things astral travelers notice is that they no longer have any need to breathe. This can be a little alarming at first, but there's a lot to get used to when you go out of body. Contrary to popular belief, you do have sensations in the astral body. You can feel heat and cold, pleasure and pain. You can hear, smell, and see. All your senses are available, including taste.

In fact, one of the perks of going out of body is that you can eat as much as you want of anything you want, and not gain a single pound.

When I first heard about astral food, I was intrigued. According to Stephen LaBerge, many of his lucid dream respondents claimed to be able to create feasts of food, upon which they would gorge with no fears of overeating or gaining weight.

This seemed like a great idea. And what better way to deal with my overly dominant desire body and my grocery store fixation?

I Eat Astral Ice Cream

I'm lucid and as I look around me, I see a grocery store coalesce into pristine reality. I am able to contain my destructive impulses, and instead I whip open the glass freezer door and pull out a large-sized container of Neapolitan ice cream.

I tear off the cap and using two fingers, scoop out a portion and eat it. It tastes cool and very chocolatey, with strawberry and vanilla. I can taste each flavor distinctly. The ice cream melts in my mouth. As I swallow it, it seems to disappear halfway down my throat.

Amazed by how good the ice cream tastes, I start bingeing. I scoop out bite after bite and put it in my mouth. It tastes so incredibly good and totally real. It's not very cold, but there is a definite subtle coolness. The taste is also slightly subdued, but still very delicious.

I continue gorging until the entire container is nearly gone. I am laughing because I can eat as much as I want and have no ill effects. Thank you, Stephen LaBerge! (December 31, 1995)

Now that I had learned how to eat dream-food, I couldn't get enough. More and more out-of-body experiences began with me creating food to eat. The cravings were overpowering, and I felt like I had to satisfy my desire body before I could get on to nobler pursuits.

While I still struggled with the desire to destroy everything in the store, now I also had to deal with wanting to consume everything too!

Astral Juice and Potato Chips

I'm lucid. I'm in Alpha Beta supermarket and even though everything looks totally real, I know it is a projection. I am delighted. I rush down an aisle and pull out a jar of orange juice. I violently rip off the cap and start guzzling down the orange juice. The taste is very subtle, and not as vivid as real life.

Disappointed, I look for something else to satisfy my

appetite. I see a bag of sour cream and onion potato chips. I tear open the bag, pull out a handful of chips, and stuff them in my mouth. They are incredibly crunchy and delicious. I take the whole bag and pour it down my throat. I eat more chips than is humanly possibly, and they taste absolutely fantastic.

As I chomp down the chips, I am shocked to see Ellen DeGeneres. The shock of seeing her nearly makes me lose lucidity. I use the spinning technique, and am just barely able to maintain awareness. As I'm chewing, I wonder about my body in bed. Is my physical mouth chewing? These chips taste so real. I wake up. (February 7, 1996)

My efforts to appease my desire body were not always successful and sometimes led to amusing situations.

I Eat Astral Wood Chips

I am lucid. I see a table. My desire body takes control and I become obsessed with the idea of eating food. I want to create a feast and chow down. I command food to appear, but nothing happens. I can't seem to think of any specific food, and after a few more tries, I become increasingly frustrated. Suddenly, I see something on the table. I reach down, scoop it up and put it in my mouth. Ugh, they are wood chips! They taste just like little chips of wood. (March 6, 1996)

Astral Peanut Butter

I'm lucid. *I must eat now!* A jar of peanut butter kindly materializes. As quickly as possible, I throw off the lid, stick in my fingers, scoop out a wad, and cram it in my mouth. Yep, it tastes and feels just like physical peanut butter. Momentarily appeased, I look around me. No surprise, I'm at my dad's house. There's my dad, but I think he's a projection. I fly through the house and into Dad's bedroom. He's sleeping in bed. I reach down and try to wake him up. He starts to move, but doesn't wake up. I suddenly feel my physical body. It is paralyzed and feels very heavy. A wave of confusion sweeps over me and I feel very thick-headed. I can't seem to shake myself into clarity. I fall asleep and wake up, energized, refreshed, and in a fantastic mood. (May 6, 1996)

Astral Skittles

I am lucid. Not having planned any specific experiments, I can't seem to think of anything at all. So I just manifest a bag of Skittles candies and eat them. They taste very sweet. (September 6, 1997)

Astral Bingeing

I'm in a car reading a map. I pick a road and take it. Suddenly, there's a shift and I'm in a place with a lot of food, either a restaurant or a kitchen. All kinds of good food is around me. I take a bite of cake. This propels me into lucidity, and I start gorging. I take big slabs of pie, cake, and ice cream and cram them into my mouth. I literally pack it in. Everything tastes incredibly real and delicious. Ice cream, bananas, chocolate, crackers, fried chicken. It tastes so real. (August 26, 2000)

According to Gnostic Samael Aun Weor and to other occult schools, one method of going out of body is to use the sexual energy. This is the key to kundalini, with which lucid dreaming is probably connected.

Patricia Garfield writes, "My present hypothesis is this: Orgasm is a natural part of lucid dreaming. My own experience convinces me that conscious dreaming is orgasmic. Too many of my students have reported similar ecstatic experiences during lucid dreams to attribute the phenomena to my individual peculiarity. There is a kind of mystic experience involved, a mini-enlightenment, when one realizes one is dreaming and can prolong the state. I believe it is quite possible that in lucid dreaming we are stimulating an area of the brain, or a chain of responses, that is associated with ecstatic states of all sorts. Sensations of flying, sexual heights, acute pleasurable awareness, and a sense of oneness are all natural outcomes of a prolonged lucid dream. . . . In fully two-thirds of my lucid dreams, I feel the flow of sexual energy; this arousal culminates in an orgasmic burst on about half these occasions" (Garfield, pp. 45, 135).

Robert Monroe also reported a sexual aspect with many of his OBEs. He often ended them with an erection, and during them had to overcome powerful sexual impulses. Garfield, on the other hand, embraced the sexual aspects of her projections. During Monroe's second projection, he was overcome by sexual feelings. As he writes, ". . . this time I experienced an overwhelmingly strong sexual drive and could think of nothing else. Embarrassed and irritated at myself because of my inability to control this tide of emotion, I returned to my physical body" (Monroe 1971, p. 30).

Monroe became quickly convinced that sex and OBEs are closely related. As he writes, "Throughout the entire experimentation, evidence began to mount of a factor most vital to the Second State [the state of OBE]. . . . This factor is sexuality and the physical sex drive. . . . There seemed to be a direct relationship between what I interpreted as the sexual drive and this 'force' that permitted me to dissociate from the physical body. Was it a redirection of this basic drive that I actually felt as 'vibrations?' Or was it the other way around? Was the sexual drive a physical and emotional manifestation of the force?" (Monroe 1971, pp. 190–195).

Monroe reports that the sexual drive was so strong in the astral dimensions that he was never able to fully overcome it. As he writes, "Instead, it was set aside, put off for the moment, while I fully recognized and acknowledged its existence" (Monroe 1971, p. 193).

I can totally relate to what Monroe is saying. Until you go out of body and feel the power of the sexual force, it's impossible to convey an accurate description.

My first really sexual lucid experience was one of the most powerful experiences of my life.

Garfield Is Right!

Suddenly, I am lucid. I am uncontrollably excited by this new development, and I leap out of my body and start running out of my room and down the hallway. I am totally thrilled. My astral body is energized, jazzed, and zinging with energy. I bound in huge leaps down the hallway. My vision is cloudy, which I've come to recognize as a sign of out-of-body vision. Otherwise, everything looks totally real.

As soon as I reach the living room, I take a step and I feel a sudden, unexpected, and hugely powerful rush of erotic feelings. I take another step and the feelings double. I am already running and can't seem to stop. With each step, I feel sexual feelings pulsing up and down my body, like a continuous orgasm. As I am running, the feelings become unbearably powerful. I have never felt anything like this in waking consciousness. I am barely able to keep running because I feel like I am in a state of constant explosion. I am still running until I become totally overwhelmed by sexual ecstasy and I slowly lose consciousness in an explosion of bliss that goes on and on. (November 4, 1989)

On occasion, erotic feelings would propel me out of my body.

Loni Anderson Kisses Me

Loni Anderson (cue!) and her friend are fighting over shoelaces (cue!). She sees me and plants a big kiss on my lips (cue!). I feel a huge rush of sexual energy and am shocked into a state of total lucidity. I know I am out of body. I jump up and try to fly through a wall. To my surprise, I can't get through it. I try again, and I bounce right off it. I just can't get through. I wake up. (July 26, 1993)

I am convinced that sex and the OBE are integrally related mainly because so many of my experiences contain this element. These experiences are still among the most powerful sexual experiences of my life.

An Erotic OBE

I feel a huge wave of erotic energy sweep through my entire body, pulling me out of my body and plunging me into a state of pure lucidity. I am elated and in a state of total ecstasy. Powerful waves of sexual energy are surging up and down my entire body. I swoop out the window in a paralyzing wave of bliss. I feel myself shatter into tiny bits and lose consciousness. (October 5, 1991)

Although erotic feelings have often prompted OBEs, occasionally the have also ended them.

Kissed by a Man

I'm suddenly lucid. Looking around me I can see that I'm in the parking lot of a nearby bookstore. It's daylight, and there are people and cars. Everything looks normal, but I sense that it's a projection.

I see a van and run up to it and try to jump through it. Instead, I squish into the side and then bounce off. My consciousness must not be very good.

Suddenly I notice a black man watching me. I run up to him. To my shock, he kisses me. I feel a rush of erotic feelings and am jolted out of lucidity and wake up. (March 16, 1996)

As time went on, I continued to feel compelled to satisfy my desire body with food and/or sex.

Vee Van Dam wrote that he had good enough control in the dream state to be able to create fully lifelike people with whom he could intimately interact. I also came to experience an increase in control, but I'm not sure if this was good news or not because now I was able to construct more elaborate scenarios and choose whomever I wanted to have sex with. That kind of temptation is hard to resist.

I Have Sex with C–

I am lucid. I fly out of body, and for some reason, I feel compelled to fly to my office. Once there, I see my coworker, C—. She looks beautiful and I am overcome with desire. I ask her if she wants to make love. She can't seem to decide, so I grab her and kiss her. She says "Yes," and we do. Man, does it feel good. (March 13, 1997)

I Make Astral Love

I'm lucid. I'm in a very large room, like an auditorium. I see a naked woman and I feel a rush of sexual energy. I try to walk and find great difficulty moving. The energy is too intense, and yet I can't control myself. I rush up to the lady and we engage in sex. Afterwards, I hear a voice, which for some reason I think is an angel. The voice says enigmatically, "My angel sent me to teach you this lesson." (April 1, 1997)

Food and Sex

Somebody grabs my butt and I feel a strong rush of sexual energy. I am catapulted into lucidity. I become obsessed with eating and I create a bunch of M&Ms. I gobble them down. They are delicious. I start to feel a little fuzzy-headed so I spin around. I am able to maintain lucidity for only a few moments until I fall into a normal dream where I am wandering inside a bookstore. (April 6, 1997)

Food and Sex

I feel the vibrations and a feeling of lightheadedness. I realize I'm lucid. Looking around me, I'm in a city environment. There are lots of buildings, streets, cars—looks very realistic. I fly down onto the sidewalk next to two young ladies. I look at them and tell them that they are my dream characters and not real. They don't believe me, so I fly away.

I fly around for several minutes, looking for someplace interesting to land. I see some telephone wires. Intrigued, I fly through them, but feel no effect. I see a gift shop and land down inside it. I examine the shelves. I see novelty key chains, little stuffed animals, toys, and other objects. On the edge of the shelf is a big slice of cheese pizza. I grab it and stuff the entire piece in my mouth. It's steaming hot and tastes great, but my whole mouth is now crammed full of food. I'm having trouble chewing and feel a mild choking sensation.

Suddenly, my mouth is empty and the desire to eat is gone. I look around the store and wonder if it is real or a projection. I try transforming objects in the store, but nothing will change. I fly up and around until I enter a large building. I fly up through the ceiling.

Is this building under construction? There are all kinds of strange plastic barriers I have to push my way through. I keep going upwards, pushing my way through the plastic barriers. I can't seem to get out. Instead of going up, I trying punching my way through a side wall. I finally pop out and I'm floating in space.

I have been lucid so long that I'm beginning to forget details. I start recalling the details, but I feel myself losing awareness so I stop thinking and concentrate on staying in the moment.

I shout out, "Take me to a healing place!" Nothing happens.

The scene shifts and I'm on the sidewalk at night, still in the city. I see somebody on the street. I decide to strip her naked and have sex with her. The scene fades so I spin and the scene comes back to life. The person is lying there naked, but I am losing awareness. I fall asleep. (August 10, 2000)

The Desire Body

I'm lucid. I create a grocery store and go crazy. I eat potato chips and guzzle soda. I create a woman and have wild sex with her. (December 27, 2000)

Creating Lovers

I'm lucid. I'm in Dad's backyard. I spin to erase illusion, but everything remains stable. I call out, "No illusion," and again, nothing happens. I fly up and into the next plane, where I start creating various people to have sex with. I'm getting pretty good at this. (August 17, 2002)

None of my sexual OBEs have resulted in the so-called wet dream. Unlike Monroe, I have not yet been able to put aside these feelings. Instead, I find that if I submit to my desires, then I get them out of the way. And as time goes on, I find that I no longer am compelled to satisfy base desires. They are simply slowly fading away.

7

Mantra Experiences

There are countless methods to achieve the out-of-body state. One of the most unusual methods is chanting mantras. Samael Aun Weor was a man who claimed to have achieved the ability to travel out of body. He left behind a legacy of teachings that have generated a following of modern Gnostics. The main focus of the teachings is to teach students how to attain the out-of-body state.

One method Weor provided is a particular mantra that the student is supposed to pronounce during the dream state. Weor called this mantra "the dynamite of the dream state." The mantra is *gaom-raom-om-bour-bu-mama-papa*. The pronunciation doesn't seem to be important. I had no experience at all with mantras and was somewhat skeptical. After all, how could a mantra have any effect? I couldn't understand the mechanics behind it, and found it hard to believe. But I was (barely) open-minded enough to try it, and knowing the power of thought on the astral plane, I thought it might prove interesting.

It sounded ridiculous to me, but I decided to give it a try. As I lay in bed one morning, I felt myself beginning to wake up. I knew I had about two seconds of lucidity, so I quickly repeated the mantra.

The second I finished the last syllable, I was plunged headlong into a bizarre state of consciousness. I felt my body begin pulsing with vibrations and become very heavy. This was followed by an energetic, whooshing rush of lucidity.

All at once, I was having about ten dreams simultaneously. I could clearly see all the different scenes playing in my mind's eye. I knew instantly that these were all dreams that I had had that night.

It was as if I had multiple streams of consciousness. All the dreams were playing out at the same time. I was overwhelmed and as the dreams continued, I tried desperately to remember all of them. But there was no way. As I frantically observed, I could see that I was forgetting about half of the dreams.

After a few moments, the ordeal was over, and I woke up. Although I was unable to recall much of what happened, I did manage to record no fewer than six separate dreams. Most were normal dreams. One was a long, powerful erotic dream. In another, my brother and I stole a park bench. In another, I traveled to France, where I spoke the language fluently. In a fourth dream, I met my obligatory celebrity, this time Fred Savage from *The Wonder Years*.

There were cues in each of these dreams to become lucid, but for whatever reason, I'm lousy at recognizing lucid cues. Only two of the dreams are presented here because they had unusual qualities. The fifth was precognitive, and the sixth was a mutual dream shared with my sister.

A Brand-New Helmet

I'm sitting on the couch in the living room when someone hands me a bright, shiny, red plastic helmet. It's brand-new and has little ridges around the edge. I try to put it on, but it's way too small. It's obviously made for a child. (December 12, 1990)

On a Cement Pathway

I'm down by the Pacific Coast on a long, narrow strip of cement, like a pathway. It's all wet, as if it had been raining. Jamey, Victoria, and I walk up the path. It's so narrow we all walk in single file. After a while, we come to a cliff area, and we have to inch along, holding hands so we won't fall. Finally, we reach an area where there is a large cage. I look inside and am shocked to see a man who has two faces! (December 12, 1990)

Having remembered six dreams that morning, I knew that they would affect my day. Of course, I never know for sure which dreams are going to contain valid information, and it always comes as a shock when the moment of waking lucidity strikes and a dream comes true.

That day, Susanne approached me and said, "Guess what I bought for James for Christmas."

"I don't know," I shrugged. "What did you get him?"

She pulled an object out of a bag, and there was a bright red plastic helmet. I recognized it instantly from my dream. In this case, the details were exactly correct, even down to the little ridges on the side of the helmet. It wouldn't be the last time I had foreknowledge of gifts.

Later that day, I talked to my sister Victoria and told her that she was in my dream that morning. I told her the dream. She looked at me in shock and told me that she had also had a very similar dream. In her dreams, she was down by the Pacific Coast when she saw a long narrow strip, which she perceived to be a river. She walked along it for a while. It was raining very hard, and suddenly she found herself on a cliff. She was forced to inch along a narrow path until she came to an area where there was a large metal chain-link fence. Big boulders came crashing down behind the fence.

We marveled at the similarity of our dreams, which shared at least seven separate elements, including the location along the coast, a narrow strip or pathway, raining, on a cliff, inching along, afraid of falling, and a chain-link fence/cage.

After that first experience with the mantra I was, of course, eager to try it again.

Deciding you want to say a mantra while lucid-dreaming or out of body is a lot easier than actually doing it. My next opportunity came about four years later. As with the first time, the mantra worked like a charm.

Out of Body!

I am lucid. I instantly think of the mantra and pronounce it out loud, *"gaom-raom-om-bour-bu-mama-papa."*

With an audible whoosh, I am propelled out of my body at high velocity. I am totally awake. It's daytime and I am hovering over the horse corral in front of my father's house. Everything is totally real. I am amazed at how well the mantra works.

I fly forward and hover in front of the horses. I wonder if they can see me. Apparently they can, because they suddenly jump up, snort, and gallop wildly away.

I wonder if I scared them and I feel a little bad. Looking around me, I wonder if I am out of body, or if this is a lucid dream. I just can't tell for sure. (September 25, 1994)

Two years later, I had another experience with the mantra.

Gaom-Raom-Om-Bour-Bu-Mama-Papa

I'm lucid. It's daytime and I am in Dad's bedroom. I feel the rush of lucidity, and as usual, the environment around me brightens and kind of fluoresces into a preternatural vividness. I am completely entranced by the beautiful greens, blues, and turquoises of his bedspread. They are much more vivid and deep than I've ever seen in the physical world. It takes me a few moments to draw my attention away from the colors.

I finally look away and remember the mantra. I pronounce out loud, *gaom-raom-om-bour-bu-mama-papa*. I am amazed at the quality of my voice, which sounds very loud and gravelly.

I feel a whoosh, and I am being pulled out of the environment. Suddenly, I am remembering four dreams at once. I am waking up. As I wake up, I frantically try to remember everything that's happening. I am splitting into four consciousnesses.

After a moment, I wake up, amazed and full of energy. As I write down the dreams, I know I have lost more than half the information. (January 22, 1996)

By this point, I was a bit in awe of this mantra. Although I had no idea how it worked or why, it was undeniably powerful. The nickname "dynamite of the dream-state" was no exaggeration. This thing works, and well.

Its effects are wide and varied. It not only works to enhance your memory, giving you essentially a download of everything that you experienced that evening while out of body, but it can also propel you into a major, high-level OBE.

My next experience with the mantra occurred just over a week later.

The Mantra Propels Me into an OBE

I am lucid. Before even looking around, I jump into the air and fly around. I can now see that I'm in a room I don't recognize. I can't tell if it's a bedroom or a living room. Could this be an office? I am having some trouble observing and remembering.

I find a mirror and stand in front of it. I don't see anything, but I remember the mantra. I say out loud "Ga—!" No sooner do I say the first syllable of the mantra than my astral body is grabbed by a terrific force and pulled sharply outside through a window.

I find myself in the clear blue sky. I am totally aware and out of body and in a delicious state of consciousness. I feel great, light, and full of lucid energy. I call out, "Hello!" but I am totally alone.

I start to lose my sight, so I concentrate on remaining conscious. I am delighted when I feel an onrush of increased lucidity. I keep flying around. Everything is bright, sunny, and beautiful.

As I fly, I think again that if people knew how great this was, they would drop everything and go out of body. I keep flying and flying. It is incredible fun. I'm thinking of all the extreme sports I've done recently, skiing, snowboarding, kayaking, mountain biking—none of them come even close to the excitement and rush of flying out of body.

I am having intense fun as I fly. I'm still in the clear blue sky, flying over my condo. I can't believe how long I stay conscious. My lucidity remains strong, and I fly for another fifteen minutes until I'm totally free and refreshed and feeling as great as I ever have. I wake up zinging with energy and in a fantastic mood. (February 4, 1996)

The power of thought on the astral plane is intense. And the more intense the thought, the more intense will be the manifestation. One experiment that I recommend everyone to try was first suggested by well-known philosopher P. D. Ouspensky.

This experiment involves a very simple command: your own name. According to Ouspensky, "a man can never pronounce his own name in sleep." As he says, "If I pronounced my name in sleep, I immediately woke up."

Garfield conducted this experiment. During a lucid dream, she began to carve her own name on a doorway. As she states, "I proceeded to do just that on the door where I was already carving. I read it and realized why Ouspensky believed it is impossible to say one's name in a lucid dream; the whole atmosphere vibrated and thundered and I woke up . . . it is not impossible to say one's own name in a lucid dream, but it is disruptive" (LaBerge and Rheingold 1985, p. 113).

A student of lucid dreamer and researcher Celia Green also conducted this experiment. As she writes, "I thought of Ouspensky's criterion of repeating one's own name. I achieved a sort of gap-in-consciousness of two words: but it seemed to have some effect; made me 'giddy,' perhaps; at any rate I stopped" (LaBerge and Rheingold 1985, p. 113).

Stephen LaBerge conducted this experiment, but his results were not nearly as dramatic. "Beyond hearing my own voice, nothing happened." He concluded that prior expectations might have influenced those who did have dramatic results.

I had tried this experiment, with little or no reaction. However, on one occasion, the results were astonishing.

I Say My Name Out of Body

I feel a strong wave of lightheadedness and become lucid. I feel very dizzy and light. I become a little confused. I see people around me and explain to them that I'm lucid. Suddenly, I realize the uselessness of trying to convince dream characters, and I feel a slight increase in awareness.

Time to experiment! I remember that something amazing is supposed to happen if you say your name while out of body. I say out loud, "My name is Preston Dennett."

There's a shift. Suddenly, I'm outside in a field in the country. It's nighttime and the sky is filled with stars. I examine the night sky and am shocked to see the most dramatic astronomical display I've ever seen. Huge fireballs are crisscrossing the night sky. It's a fantastic meteor shower. The effect is incredible, and I am totally awestruck.

I fly upwards and into the sky. I keep going up until suddenly there's a shift and I'm in another dimension. I'm surrounded by millions of tiny, shiny, golden flakes. It's like being inside a ball filled with gold glitter. It is indescribably beautiful. I feel absolutely fantastic.

There's a shift and I end up in another place, which I can't quite remember. (March 19, 1997)

After more than ten years of practice, I finally reached a level where I could confidently say that I was no longer a novice. I could achieve the out-of-body state on a fairly regular basis, about once a week. I was able to maintain consciousness, control my thoughts and emotions, and initiate a wide variety of experiments. I had learned how to move and how to see.

I was finally ready for some more serious research.

8

OBEs and Healing

Many OBE travelers have had experiences with miraculous healings. Robert Monroe reports receiving healing energies. Albert Taylor writes that his symptoms of multiple sclerosis disappeared, possibly as a result of his travels. Marilyn Hughes was able to effect several cures. Robert Bruce cured himself of a medical problem with his hip. Bruce Moen gives a particularly moving and vivid account of how he was able to cure himself of a rare liver disease using OBEs. Paul Twitchell cured himself of a serious childhood illness. Terrill Wilson woke up after a powerful OBE and was healed of a bad cold. As he writes, "Lo and behold, my fever, nausea, sore throat, and head congestion were completely gone. Upon waking the next morning, the only trace of sickness in me was a slight sniffle" (Wilson, p. 104).

A personal friend of mine had a near-death experience in which she was actually cured of cancer. So I knew that healings could be done with OBEs. However, I never had the opportunity.

Then, in 2000, I began to experience a series of pains in my arms and legs. These pains were random and went away after a few days so I wasn't overly concerned. However, in 2001, I experienced excruciating pain in my left wrist and hand. I was convinced I had developed carpal tunnel syndrome from excessive mountain biking. Then the pain moved up to my elbow and back, and I started to feel really terrible.

I went to the doctor and got the shock of my life. I was diagnosed with rheumatoid arthritis. Today it is largely in remission. I've managed to keep the disease in control through the use of medication and possibly because of some of the following experiences.

Before I was diagnosed, I had pain only in my left arm and didn't know the cause. I knew about healing with OBEs, so I tried to heal myself.

OBE Healing

Marco calls my name and it wakes me up (false awakening). I am so tired I fall back asleep and wake up out of body. I break through the screen window and climb through it. I can barely see, so I shout out, "Clarity!" several times until I am totally conscious. I am in the field directly east of my father's house. While there is normally a house there, the field is empty. I lie down in the field and start rolling in the dry grass. It's very noisy and crackly.

Then I remember my intention to heal my arm. I grab my left arm and look at it. It looks beautiful, normal, fleshy-pink, and healthy. I grip it tightly with my right hand and repeat fervently, "Heal! Heal! Heal!" until I lose consciousness. (April 14, 2001)

A few weeks later, my arm was still hurting. Still thinking that I had carpal tunnel syndrome, I tried another attempt at healing myself.

You Must Climb into Your Crown

I'm lucid. I shout out, "Clarity! Clarity! Clarity!" I feel a strong rush of swirling and pulsing energy. I hold it, increase the flow, and when it reaches a certain threshold, I flop out of my body. I carefully open my eyes and I can see a muddled jumble of colors and shapes. It clarifies until I can see that I'm outside on a pathway. I shout out, "Clarity!" until I'm fully conscious. Then I grab my arm and I command, "Heal! Heal! Heal!"

I don't feel any reaction, so instead of demanding for a healing to take place, I decide to take another strategy. Looking around me, I see that I am outside in a field. I am standing along a pathway. I see a beautiful lady with long dark hair and fair skin on the path ahead; she is looking at me. She's thin and is wearing a dress. She is beautiful. I don't know if she's real or a projection, but either way, I'm hoping she can help me. I rush up to her and ask, "What can I do to heal myself?" My voice comes out low and gravelly, but clear enough.

The lady looks at me and quietly and calmly replies, "You must climb into your crown."

I listen carefully and am pretty certain I hear her correctly, but I don't quite understand what she means. My crown? My head? Climb? I repeat the phrase several times to be sure and remember it.

Looking around, I see a man. I rush up to him and ask the same question. However, before he can answer, I wake up. (May 6, 2001)

I had no idea what the message was supposed to mean. Later I received the helpful hint from a friend that it might mean activating my crown chakra. After he said that, it seemed so obvious. In any case, my wrist still hurt. A few days later, I had the following experience.

My Hands!

I'm lucid on the stairway of my condo building. I see Christy. I tell her, "I'm lucid and so are you!" She rolls her eyes in disbelief.

Suddenly, for no reason I can imagine, I shout out, "My hands!" At that second, I hold them over my head or they are somehow lifted upwards. I feel a strong, buzzing electrical force in my hands, like they were being dipped in electrical water. The force is powerful and unexpected, but I sense that it is a healing force.

Wondering if I'm out of body, I spin to erase illusion. Suddenly I'm spinning at super-high speeds and I feel a strong pressure behind both eyeballs. It is almost painful. I become concerned and stop. I am promptly pulled back into my body. I feel the vibrations and am propelled out again, but I fall quickly into a normal dream. (May 11, 2001)

I was surprised by this OBE because both my hands were pulled up, yet I was experiencing pain only in one hand. A few weeks later, however, the pain spread to both arms and I was given my diagnosis.

A Healing Place

I wake up out of body. I'm walking around in my bedroom. As soon as I realize I'm out of body, I fly up and out the window. I pop out at my father's house. I carefully observe the environment. It looks realistic. I feel a cool breeze flowing (first time I have felt the wind during an OBE) and notice that my astral body is swaying slightly. I shout out, "Take me to a healing place!"

The environment doesn't change but suddenly I can feel heat permeating my body, an actual warmth. I am amazed at how physical it feels. (September 23, 2001)

Out-of-Body Physical Therapy

I'm dreaming when I suddenly become lucid. The scene shifts and I'm out of body in my living room. Awareness slowly floods into me until I have a full waking awareness. I examine my living room, carefully noting details. I am delighted because my awareness is very sharp, I can see perfectly, and I have excellent control. I start singing loudly. My voice is so loud that I wonder if my physical body is singing. I reach up and feel my vocal cords, but there is no vibration. I create a piece of bread and eat it. It sort of sticks in my throat and I swallow it.

I fly into my bathroom and create a mirror. I see my reflection. I look normal. At age 38, I've lost most of my hair. As I watch, my hair comes streaming back, long and luxuriant. My skin smoothens and I lose about fifteen years of age in a few seconds. I look so incredibly young. Amused, I fly back into my living room.

Suddenly, I remember my arthritis and my desire to heal myself. I am suddenly ecstatic because I feel no pain at all. I am totally free of pain. The feeling is a huge relief and is absolutely exquisite. This is how I want to feel in the physical. I must heal myself. Knowing that the astral body is superior to the physical body, I start exercising furiously. I do jumping jacks and start shadow-boxing and moving in ways which would normally hurt my left elbow. My arm feels great and I have full movement. I keep swinging and stretching in the hopes that these movements will translate into the health of my physical body. (January 25, 2003)

Unfortunately, I still have symptoms of RA, but virtually all progress of the disease appears to have stopped. I wouldn't be at all surprised if some of my OBEs have helped in my healing, and I remain confident that I can be healed through out-of-body travel. I will keep trying.

9

Meetings with God and My Higher Self

I had been able to conduct a number of experiments and explorations. I was able to reach the conscious out-of-body state regularly. I was able to maintain lucidity and control my out-of-body emotional outbursts to some degree. I became able to move beyond the lower physical dimensions and solicit experiences of a much higher vibrational level.

Nearly all the advanced out-of-body travelers speak of traveling to the higher dimensions, meeting with God, their Higher Selves, and other spiritual beings. This sounded like great fun, and feeling up to the challenge, I was determined to reach for the stars. Although I did have certain expectations about what would happen, I was invariably surprised by the results.

During a lucid dream, Stephen LaBerge decided to "seek the highest." It turned into one of the most profound and mystical experiences of his life, yet one that is typical of advanced projectors. In the experience, he flew upwards into the clouds, where he saw various religious symbols. Writes LaBerge, "As I rose still higher, beyond the clouds, I entered a vast mystical realm: a vast emptiness that was yet full of love; an unbounded space that somehow felt like home" (LaBerge and Rheingold 1985, p. 270).

Researcher Fariba Bogzaran conducted a study of people who seek God or their Higher Selves while in the lucid state. Her study found that 80 percent of those who believed in a "personal God" experienced God represented as a person, while 80 percent of those who believed in an "impersonal Deity" experienced God as something other than a person (LaBerge and Rheingold 1985, p. 240).

Robert Peterson tried this experiment on several occasions. During one OBE, he felt as if he was in the presence of Jesus Christ. During another OBE, he saw images of spiders, and in another, galaxies. During yet another OBE, he asked specifically to see God. As he writes, "Almost at once, a single bolt of energy came shooting down from above and hit me. The force of the energy bolt was so powerful that it knocked my astral body to the ground. It was just raw power; there was no feeling behind it . . . it was more like I had touched an energy force too powerful for me to handle" (Peterson 2001, pp. 97–98).

Robert Monroe and Bruce Moen also report encountering both their Higher Selves and later a God-like entity. And certainly many NDEers claim to have met God as represented by the Light.

A personal friend (a computer programmer) took my advice during a lucid dream and shouted out, "Take me to see God!" He found himself hurtling through outer space until he landed in a room filled with a vast array of computers. At the center console was a little old man operating the entire computer system, which he felt represented the universe.

While it seems clear that preconceptions may influence this type of mystical experience, or that symbols play a powerful role, I was very curious to see what my experiences would be. I'm definitely not religious, and I really had no idea what to expect God or my Higher Self to be like. I was so puzzled by what happened that I ended up seeking the experience over and over.

Going to Meet God

I am with Karen in a bunk bed in my room. I am confused because I don't have a bunk bed, and Karen shouldn't be here. Suddenly, I accidentally fall out of bed. As I hit the floor, I become totally lucid. I stand up, and looking around me, I can see that I'm out of body. It is still dark out, and although I can see clearly and everything looks normal, it is very dark. I am now in my bedroom.

Feeling a rush of energy, I am unable to stay still and leap out of my bedroom into the living room. I am chanting over and over, "I'm dreaming! I'm dreaming! I'm dreaming!" Even though I know I'm out of body, this works well to maintain my awareness.

I am in the living room, but it's so dark, I still can't make out much. Knowing I should have some measure of control, I shout out "Light! Light!" Nothing happens. I repeat loudly, "Let there be light!"

Despite being as biblically commanding as I can be, nothing happens and it remains totally dark. I realize that I can't change the light level because I'm not lucid-dreaming, I'm out of body.

Disappointed, I walk towards my balcony. Suddenly, I remember the other experiment I wanted to try: saying my name. Feeling very curious about what will happen, I say out loud, "I'm Preston."

My voice sounds normal, but to my surprise, nothing happens. Thinking I must not have said it loud enough, or that I need to say my surname also, I shout out, "My name is Preston Dennett!"

To my disappointment, nothing happens. I'm thinking that Ouspensky didn't know what he was talking about; you can say your name and nothing spectacular will happen.

It's obvious to me that I am wasting precious time and energy, so I decide to do a really bold experiment. Some people who have gone out of body claim to have met highly spiritual beings, including Jesus and even God. What do I have to lose?

With all the will I can muster, I say forcefully and out loud, "I want to see my God!"

Suddenly, I feel my astral body gripped by an extremely powerful force, and I am quickly whisked straight upwards and though the ceiling. The shock is so great that I instantly lose consciousness. I wake up sometime later. (February 28, 1993)

I woke up from this experience feeling incredibly refreshed and totally energized. It was hard to remember the last time I had been in such a great mood. I felt so good. I was finally being rewarded for all my hard work. I was disappointed that I couldn't stay awake long enough to see what happened after I called on God, but I was delighted by how far I got. I could always try again.

More than four years passed before I was able to make another attempt. I was totally shocked by the outcome of this out-of-body experience and it took me years before I could understand it. I'm not sure if I do even today.

I Call on My Higher Self

I'm having an erotic dream when the sexual energy suddenly becomes overpowering and I am electrified into lucidity and propelled out of my body. I fly out onto my balcony. Looking up, I see what looks like a balloon. I reach up to grab it, but I can't quite reach it. I jump off the balcony, and I am floating in midair. The balloon disappears and I realize that I am totally out of body. The balloon was a tricky device to get me fully lucid.

I know exactly what I want to do. I give the command, "I want to see my Higher Self!" My astral body jerks violently, and I am hurtling upwards at high speeds. I break through a barrier and I am deposited at the end of a long, dark hallway with a door at the end. I know that beyond this door is my Higher Self.

I am very excited. I rush down the hallway. There are no

other doors. It looks like an old apartment building. I am very excited and have no idea what I am about to see. I fling open the door.

I am amazed at what I see. It's a small room, maybe ten by twelve feet. I don't notice any windows. There is paneling on the walls, and there are several bookcases filled with books, bottles, miniature statues, knickknacks, and lots of other neat stuff. There is a desk and a nice chair. Every shelf and drawer are filled with all kinds of things. I am totally intrigued.

But I am mostly shocked by whom I see in the room. It is my brother Marco and his wife, Christy. They are both waiting for me. Both of them are smiling with expressions of amusement. I laugh uproariously and tell them, "Guess what, you guys are my Higher Self!" For some reason, I find this idea incredibly funny.

I examine the room more closely. I see a mirror on one wall. I rush up to it and look at my reflection. I am shocked by what I see. I look like myself, except my face and eyes are distorted. My skin looks tight, and my eyes have taken on a distinctly Asian appearance. I gaze at my reflection until I lose consciousness. (March 22, 1997)

My next attempt to contact my Higher Self yielded similarly strange results.

Show Me My Higher Self!

I am lucid. I feel the vibrations. I am imagining myself rising up and down, as if on the bow of a ship moving through the waves. I suddenly recognize that William Buhlman recommended this as a method to go out of body. As soon as I realize this, I pop fully out of my body. I am flying around, but I am having great difficulty seeing.

I shout out, "Clarity! Clarity! Clarity!" to improve my sight, and I feel a wave of high awareness sweep over me, though my sight remains dim.

I shout out, "Show me my Higher Self!" Suddenly, there's a shift and I'm in the backyard of my dad's house. My dad's friend Diane is standing underneath the eucalyptus tree with a male friend of hers whom I don't even know.

I am shocked and confused. I like Diane a lot, even love her. I babysat her son, and she used to drive me to school. But is she really my Higher Self? She looks at me smiling and says, "I think you've got the wrong person."

I laugh. What could this possibly mean, I wonder? I have no idea. Seeking further experience, I fly up and say, "Take me to Christy's house."

I zoom quickly over the mountains and across the San Fernando Valley. I am halfway to her house when I happen to fly over my former junior high school. As soon as I see it, I'm instantly standing in the playground courtyard. I fly through the open entryways between the classrooms until I end up at the school cafeteria.

I see a big plate of macaroni and cheese. Uh-oh, I know what this means. I must eat. I gobble it down. It tastes great. (June 1, 1997)

(The next day, my friend Judy called me up and invited me over for dinner. I was not surprised to find that she was serving macaroni and cheese. By this point, I was having precognition of many events in my life.)

My next attempt at contacting my Higher Self produced even stranger results. At the same time, I think it provided a possible clue as to what these OBEs were trying to tell me.

I Meet My Higher Self

I'm suddenly aware that I am out of body, floating about two feet above my bed. I shout out, "Take me to see my Higher Self!"

I am instantly propelled upwards through my ceiling and into the sky above my condo. There's a momentary blur of color and a feeling of intense forward motion, and I find myself in a small room.

It looks like a typical business office. Thick, plush carpet covers the floor. The walls are paneled. A small couch is against the wall near the door. At the other end is a large wood desk with just a few files on top. My attention is instantly drawn to the lady sitting behind the desk.

She's pretty, with longish blond hair and a round face. She's not skinny, but in no way is she fat either. A nice figure. She's well dressed in a conservative outfit. She's obviously waiting for me. She has her hands folded patiently across her desk. When I walk in, she looks at me and smiles with a hint of mischief.

She's just looking at me, smiling knowingly, not saying a word. I somehow know that her name is Bonnie. (Or is it Susan?) I think she's a real person—I can tell by her presence—but I have no idea who she is. I am incredulous and look at her thinking, "You are my Higher Self? I don't know you."

She just keeps staring at me with a pleasant, mischievous smile. (November 10, 1997)

I was confused by the results of these experiences. Something different happened each time. I had no idea what I expected to see when I called on my Higher Self, but it certainly wasn't other people. And every time I called on God, it either didn't work, or I was gripped by a force too powerful for me. Could it be that my Higher Self is other people? Maybe we are all connected. Could this be what my experiences are trying to say?

I will definitely try to visit my Higher Self and God again.

10

High-Level Out-of-Body Experiences

Although rarely, I have on occasion had what I consider to be mystical out-of-body experiences, in which I have been able to access what I believe to be higher dimensions.

As any advanced astral traveler will tell you, there appear to be different planes or dimensions. All of this is carefully mapped out in various Eastern religions, and astral travelers like Robert Monroe, William Buhlman, Robert Bruce, Bruce Moen, Marilyn Hughes, Robert Peterson, and many others have made significant explorations into these higher dimensions.

My first experience with a high-level astral projection was comparatively brief. Nevertheless, it remains one of the most profound spiritual experiences of my life.

Out of Body and the Place of Knowledge
Lucid! I fly out of my body and run into my living room, out onto my balcony, and leap into the air. I am floating outside

my condo, totally awake, and sure that I am out of body. Looking around, I see it is early morning. Everything looks totally real. I fly around and up over my condo, until I am a few hundred feet above it.

I am so incredibly conscious. Looking across the horizon, I can see the buildings of downtown Los Angeles and the rising Santa Monica Mountains. I can't resist, and in an instant I am flying at high speeds over the San Fernando Valley to downtown L.A. I fly over and around several of the tall buildings and then fly away and over the Santa Monica Mountains.

My astral body is zinging with energy and I can't believe how wonderful and freeing it feels to fly this way. I swoop down over the countryside, flying and turning and doing all sorts of maneuvers. I can't believe I'm still conscious. Usually after flying this long, I can't sustain the zinging energies.

I keep flying until I suddenly see my condo as a little white dot down below me. I swoop down and finally come back to my balcony, where I land softly.

I float through the closed sliding glass door without any sensation and float above the couch. I am more conscious than I ever remember being, and all that flying has left my astral body zinging with energy. I feel great!

I am sitting there totally absorbed in soaking up the refreshing energies. I am thinking that I've been out of body for nearly an hour and this has got to be one of the longest times I've ever maintained consciousness.

I know I must take advantage of this and try one of my experiments. I remember reading that there are "places of knowledge" on the astral plane, secret schools where travelers can go to learn ancient wisdom.

I think to myself "Go to a place of knowledge!"

Suddenly I feel a strong pull on my astral body and I am pulled upwards at high velocity through my roof and into outer space. I start going faster and faster and the physical world around me slowly disappears. This goes on for at least a few minutes. I am thinking that this is taking a very long time, and I begin to feel concerned that I might be getting too far away from my body. I can't see anything because I'm moving so fast. I decide to stop, turn around, and fly back.

I stop and look around. I'm having a lot of trouble focusing. I kind of shake my head and blink, and this clears my vision. Looking around me, I am a tiny speck floating in a huge, vast, open area. I am the tiniest dot floating on the edge of an enormous black tunnel-looking thing. There are lots of foggy patches and wide, dark holes or caverns stretching in an incredible vastness on all sides.

Everything looks very interdimensional with no solid features or anything remotely familiar. I am intrigued and wonder where I am. Slowly, the scene begins to transform.

As I watch, a totally lifelike environment coalesces around me. I am totally fascinated to find myself in a normal-looking dirt field. It is daytime. There are other people around, trees, a road. I am wondering if this is a park and what this all means, when I look up and see something of extraordinary beauty.

High above me in the sky are two small, glowing spheres. One is pure gold, the other pure silver. They are glowing and reflecting with exquisite beauty. I look at them and feel an intense emotional pull. They are the most beautiful things I have ever seen in my entire life, and my entire soul, every inch of my being, aches to have them.

As I stare at them, I know exactly what they represent. As they hover there high in the sky, I know they are for me, that they are a gift meant especially for me. I know that they mean one thing: my eventual spiritual enlightenment.

I have never wanted anything so badly in my entire life.

Still in total command of my waking consciousness, I calmly sit down and make a strong, fervent wish. "Please let them come to me. Please let them come to me. Please let them come to me."

I hope, pray, command, visualize, and pull with all my power to make those beautiful spheres mine.

Slowly, slowly, so slowly, the spheres drift downward. They are getting closer and closer. Soon they are within reach.

I jump up and grab them. They are mine! I can't believe it. They are mine! I am totally ecstatic and feel a hugely powerful rush of lucidity and vibrations. I feel incredibly humble and proud and relieved and fantastic as the vibrations pulse through my body. I wake up in bed, zinging with energy and feeling absolutely great. (October 7, 1994)

Near-death experiences have much in common with out-of-body experiences, the only real difference being that NDEers are out of their bodies due to trauma. However, in nearly every other respect, they seem to be identical.

One thing that interested me was the consistency of description by near-death experiences of the "Light." Described as all-loving and all-knowing, the Light is so regularly reported, that I wondered if it was possible for an OBEer to find it.

When I finally remembered to search for the Light, I was very surprised to find it.

Out of Body—in the Light

I'm lucid, out of body. It's daytime, and I'm flying around my house. It feels so great and refreshing and freeing. I love this. I keep flying and flying until I feel waves of lucid energy pulsing through my astral body. I'm really zinging and feeling great. My awareness feels especially sharp. I fly outside and into the sky and am wondering what to do next, when suddenly I see it—off in the distance—the Light.

I instantly think that this is the Light that near-death experiencers talk about. It's way off in the distance, and looks like a huge, glowing cloud. The light is bright, bright white, with a kind of warm, yellowish comforting tinge. I am instantly drawn towards it and start moving towards it.

My speed increases, but it seems to take a while to get there. The cloud of Light looms larger and larger until I am just a speck next to it. It looks like a bright sun, but whiter and warmer and more beautiful.

I am entranced and delighted and in awe. I dive into the light until it surrounds me. I'm inside the Light. Everything feels incredibly warm, soothing and wonderful. I feel great, great, great!

Suddenly, there's a shift, and I find myself in a strange room. I feel a slight loss of lucidity, and know that I have just forgotten part of what is happening to me. Looking around I see a screened window. I take my hand and thrust it through the screen. It rips strangely, and doesn't really follow the laws of physics. Still, I'm amazed at how physical and real it looks.

Suddenly, there's another shift and I'm back in my grocery store. I'm having a lot of trouble moving, and it feels like I'm stuck in molasses. I drag myself along the frozen foods section and start to ransack the place. I pull stuff off the shelves, open them, and dump the contents. I break windows and throw things across the room. I wake up in mid-throw. (December 17, 1995)

In this experience, I learned the reason for the shifts and feelings of having lost part of the memory of my experience. Each time there's a shift, it's because we are changing energy bodies. I was vibrating high enough to enter a high dimension, but at some point, I fell back into the lower vibration and into a lower energy body.

It took me a while to recognize the different astral bodies. But it becomes clear when you have to download your memory from the higher to the lower bodies and then finally the physical body. This concept became very clear because of the following experience. I consider this OBE to be one of the most profound experiences of my life, either in the body or out of it. Ever since my mother died, I have been on a quest to find out what happened to her, if there truly is life after death.

As a result of the following experience, I had answers to both my questions.

A Tour of the Heavenly Realms

I am lucid. I leap out of my body and fly into my living room. To my shock and delight, there is somebody standing in the center of the room. I realize instantly that this is a real person and not a projection. It is a beautiful black woman. She is wearing a nice dress and has long black braids, large dark eyes, and a wide smile. She is looking straight at me. I feel like I somehow know her and love her, but I have no idea who she is. I'm wondering, could she be my spirit guide? I have a million questions running through my head. I rush up to meet her.

When I reach her, she smiles at me with a hint of mischief, grabs my shoulders, spins me around, and, placing her hands squarely on my back, she pushes me forcefully through the wall.

I stumble forward and pop through the wall to the other side. I'm in another place. Still totally conscious, I look around me. It's daytime and I'm outside in a courtyard alongside a street. There are large stone tiles on the ground. There are several small marble tables with chairs surrounded by a low wrought-iron fence. Several well-dressed people are sitting at the tables, eating and chatting. Several small buildings line the street. I have no idea where this is. For some reason, it reminds me of France.

Feeling incredibly aware, I decide to try some experiments. I remember that Marco and Christy are looking for a home, so I shout out, "Take me to see Marco and Christy's future home!"

My astral body is instantly catapulted upwards and forwards. The landscape becomes a blur of color as I hurtle towards my destination at high speed. Suddenly I slow down.

I am over a typical suburb. Two-story houses are neatly lined in rows alongside small streets. I stop a few hundred feet over one particular house. This is the one!

I memorize the landscape. There is a tall stone cliff about twenty feet behind the house. Almost no backyard. A small front yard and homes on either side. A red tile roof.

I swoop down and go into the house. I land inside the hallway. I am amazed at how clear everything looks. I am doing really well with my awareness. I see the kitchen and dining room on my right, the living room on my left. There are bedrooms behind me and a staircase going down to the basement in front of me.

I am wondering if there are any mental projections so I shout out, "All illusion disappear!" Instantly at least half of the furniture disappears, as do several pictures and other things. There are only a few tables and chairs left. I laugh and fly downstairs into the basement. It is mostly empty and very spacious and clean. I fly up and out to the front yard, turn around, and examine the front of the house. I memorize the details and start floating upwards.

Then I put some power into it and start flying upwards, faster and faster. I realize that I'm not breathing and wonder about my body in bed. I'm not worried about it, so I just keep flying and wonder what to do next.

Ah, yes! I want to contact my mother. I have tried this before and it has never worked, but feeling very aware, I shout out "Mom! Mother!"

Instantly, my mother appears. I am electrified with happiness.

I am amazed by her appearance. She looks about twenty-five years old, younger than me. Her hair is light brown instead of dark. She is smiling and is as happy as I am at the reunion. We come together and hug. The feeling of love is intense.

She looks at me as if to say, "I've got a surprise for you!" She takes me by the hand and pulls me upwards. We are flying together, hand-in-hand at high speeds. I have no idea where we're going, but I'm excited to find out.

Suddenly, there's a shift and we are sitting in an American luxury car. My mother is driving and I'm in the passenger seat. I'm amazed by its sudden appearance and my mom is laughing.

Then I'm immediately transfixed by what I see outside. It is the strangest landscape I have ever seen. The entire ground is completely covered with smooth, fist-sized brown stones. The terrain stretches out into hills and flat plains for miles, but all of it is the same. The effect is stunning. There's no place like this on earth. I am wondering where we are and where we are going. My mom looks at me and smiles as if to say, "Just wait."

We travel along the thin, winding road through the rocky landscape for a few more moments when suddenly there's a shift!

We are in a different place. The car is gone and we are standing at the edge of a small field of green grass. In the distance is a forest, mountains, and green, rolling hills. There is a small creek running along the edge of the pasture. There are no signs of civilization.

The scene is straight out of postcard and looks absolutely beautiful. The sky is glowing brightly, and everything is in brilliant color. I feel incredibly great and free. I can't ever remember being in a better mood. Even the air itself seems to sparkle with love and good cheer. I never want to leave this place. I recognize the feeling and remember having been here before. This is what many people call the Heavenly realms. I am totally elated. It feels like a summer morning and all my problems have been swept away in a tide of total bliss.

Mom takes my hand and we lift up and fly across the field. We keep flying until we reach the edge of the pasture. We land next to the creek. My mom looks at me with a glint of mischief in her eyes. Then she jumps into the creek and pulls me in after her.

I laugh as we fall into the creek. As the water spills over me, I become fascinated by its feeling and texture. It feels totally real, cool, and refreshing, but it doesn't get me the slightest bit wet! It just drips instantly off my body.

My mom is laughing at my bewilderment. She reaches down and grabs a giant strand of algae and flings it at me. It hits me square in the face.

I am shocked. This is just like her to surprise me. I pull off the algae and am again amazed that it doesn't leave me dirty. My mom laughs and flings another piece at me. It hits me in the chest and neck.

Okay, this is war! I reach down, grab a handful and hurl it at her body. Even though I know it won't hurt her, I'm afraid to hit her in the face. She, however, has no such qualms and flings another piece. The algae fight goes on for a few more minutes until we are both rolling with laughter.

I am so happy. My mom looks at me and raises her eyebrows as if to say, "Just wait, you haven't seen anything yet." It's like we have a telepathic link and I know what she's thinking, or we don't need words.

She grabs me by the hand and we start flying upwards, faster and faster. Our speed increases when suddenly, there's another shift or a barrier, and we pop through it and into another place.

We are in a place of such incredible sacred pure beauty that I am completely humbled and in awe. Surrounding us is a landscape of pure white crystal, stretching for miles and miles in every direction. I can see everything in panoramic detail. The crystals are all shapes and sizes, but they are all shades of glowing white. Some are translucent, some are opaque. Some are shining with an incredible brilliance. Some are very tiny, like grains of sand. Others are the size of houses. Some are reflecting, others seem to be emitting light.

I am amazed by the quality of my vision. Not only is it panoramic, but I have the capability to zoom in on any crystal, no matter how distant, and examine it as if it were close up. I am delighted by this newfound ability and I pick various distant crystals and closely examine their facets.

This place is incredible. I have never seen anything so beautiful in all my life. No one would ever believe that such a place even existed. The feeling of cool pure peace is all-encompassing. If I thought the pastoral place we just left was Heavenly, this place is like Nirvana.

My mom is looking at me patiently, and is obviously highly amused by my awe of and reverence for this fantastic place. She is sitting perched on one of the larger crystals, sitting very regally as she did when she was alive. She is kind of joking with me, saying, "Surprised you, didn't I? What do you think of this place?"

I can only smile and shake my head. Now that she has my attention, she again raises her eyebrows and smiles, as if to say, "Watch this!"

Oh, no, I think, here we go again.

She laughs and points to a cluster of small crystals right next to us. I look at where she's pointing and watch in utter astonishment as the crystals in this small area suddenly turn bright orange. The orange patch is about two or three feet in diameter, and is darkest orange in the center.

I look at her, amazed. That was a neat trick. She smiles and motions for me to taste it. "Taste it?" I think, incredulously.

She nods and motions again, smiling. I reach down and scoop up a handful of the orange crystals and put them in my mouth. I am instantly overcome by an incredible and unique sensation. The crystals start popping and squirting in my mouth. They taste more like orange than any orange I have ever tasted. The flavor is so strong, so sweet, so pure. They kind of sizzle and pop in my mouth, exploding with intense orange flavor. The taste is almost electrically orange. It tastes so good. It's totally fantastic!

I look at my mom and pour out my thanks to her.

She smiles and takes me by the hand. It's time to go back. We fly downward and we end up back in the pastoral Heavenly realm. There are other people walking in couples or small groups along sidewalks or pathways. There are grassy green hills covered with flowers and little pathways crisscrossing the area.

Everybody is incredibly happy and serene. It's impossible to be in a bad mood in this place. We walk along the pathways for a short distance then sit down on one of the benches. I look at my mom and study her appearance. She looks so incredibly young.

She is laughing again at my expression. She then points to the sky and says, "Look!"

Written in white fluffy clouds are the words, "Love you! Love you! Love you!"

I laugh with delight and pour my love back out to her. We hug, and suddenly I know it's time for me to say goodbye. Although I don't want to leave, I'm so happy that it doesn't matter. It's time for me to go.

There's a shift and I'm suddenly flying down a tight, bright tunnel at supersonic speeds. Another shift, and I pop out in a strange room. I quickly manifest a dream journal and write down the experience. I realize that I have shifted down a dimension or body and I need to carefully record all the details of the experience or I will forget it. Once I have all the details fixed in my mind, I lie down on a dream-bed and try to wake up.

I then go through a series of false awakenings. Each time, I pause and carefully recall and memorize the experience. I am happy because I know I am remembering pretty much everything.

This happens four or five times, and each time I go through the same process of recall. I begin to get a little nervous about losing my memory of this event, and wonder how many shifts I have to go through to wake up for real. I am amazed at what a laborious process it is to step down these memories into the physical dimension.

Finally, I wake up and look around me. Am I really awake? It takes me a second to get my bearings. Yes, I'm in my bedroom. The whole experience floods into my mind. I start crying as I carefully recall all the details. I'm so exhilarated. I can't remember ever feeling so refreshed, rejuvenated. It feels like pure energy is pulsing through my body. I am so happy. (March 2, 1997)

High-level OBEs make all the hard work worth the effort. It's one thing to visit various places on earth or to fool around with the power of thought on the astral plane. However, exploring the finer dimensions is particularly fun.

A Finer Dimension

John is trying to wake me up. He grabs my bedroll and tries to drag it out of the living room while I'm still on it! He's got to be kidding! Then I realize, John would never do that. I must be dreaming. The scene flashes into surreal vividness. I'm in his living room in San Diego. I fly up and over the house and look around. I am definitely out of body.

Knowing that vast distances can be traversed instantly while out of body, I decide to fly from San Diego to Los Angeles. Suddenly, my astral body is grabbed by a strong force and I'm hurtling over the freeways at super-fast speeds. Everything blurs with high-speed movement. Seconds later, I slow down and I'm over Cheney Valley in L.A. I'm grazing the treetops and flying towards my dad's house. There it is. I hover above the house, amazed that I just traveled 150 miles in a matter of seconds. I am so incredibly awake and conscious. It's the perfect time for an experiment.

I decide to give my favorite command. I say out loud, "Take me where I need to go!"

Suddenly, my astral body is jerked upwards. I'm flying straight up at very high speeds. I'm going up, up, up.

Suddenly, the scene begins to transform. I'm in a different dimension! Looking around me, I am surrounded by beautiful, glowing clouds. I am whizzing at high speeds through dazzling layers of mists. Gold and silver tendrils miles long stream past me as I race quickly towards I-don't-know-where.

I keep looking around me in a state of total awe. I am the tiniest speck in a vast sea of gold and silver mist. It is indescribably beautiful. The energy of the place is cool and pure. I feel amazingly peaceful and serene. I have no idea where I am but I like it. I soak up the beauty and energy of the place as I keep flying. Suddenly, I pop through a barrier of some kind and I'm in another place. I look around me. Oh my God, I'm in Marco and Christy's house. This is the perfect opportunity for me to get evidence that I'm actually out of my body. I had earlier thought of looking at their chalkboard, which always has different messages on it. I decide to look for it, but I can't seem to find it. I give up that idea and start looking for something that I will remember. Then I see photographs. There are photos on either side of Marco and Christy's bed. They are on the bed tables along with a lamp, plants, a clock, and other small objects. I commit the scene to memory, telling myself over and over, "I must remember this. I will remember this. Remember this too."

I float down the hallway, looking for something else to do or look at. I try to fly through the wall and, bam! I bounce right off it. It feels totally solid, which I don't understand. I should be able to go through it.

Suddenly, there's a strong shift.

I'm in the past, maybe fifteen years ago. I'm at my dad's house. I fly down through the roof and land in the living room. I am shocked to see my mother, looking to be about age 45. James and Mudita are with her. I hug Mom, but she can't see me or feel me and doesn't know I'm there. I'm wondering if she's even real because she had died shortly after James was born, and here James looks like he's about four years old and Mudita maybe seven.

I don't understand exactly because everybody seems real to me. I'm confused about what year this is supposed to be, but I'm certain it's in the past.

I look at Mudita, and to my surprise, she seems to be looking right at me. The expression on her face is a mixture of bewilderment and alarm. I can tell she doesn't know it's me, but she sees something. She doesn't seem to know what she is seeing. I hope I'm not scaring her. I send a thought of love to her forehead. Everything slowly fades and I wake up in an incredibly good mood. (March 10, 1997)

My most extensive OBEs have occurred only when I am able to maintain my awareness while out of body. That is key. Once you are able to maintain awareness, you are able to enjoy the higher dimensions because you are already accessing them—you just don't remember.

One experiment I always wanted to try was to travel into the past and see the wreck of the *Titanic*. The results were unexpected.

In Search of the *Titanic*

I'm lucid. It's daytime and I'm driving a car down the street. I recognize the car as a mental construction that I created to account for my movement. I push off the steering wheel and fly out the side window. I'm in the sky flying around, turning sharp corners, performing loops and flips. I am totally out of body. This is one of the greatest benefits of OBEs; there is nothing quite so fun as flying. I fly for several minutes until I remember that I want to do some experiments. I remember my desire to see the *Titanic*.

I shout out, "I want to see the *Titanic!*"

Instantly, my astral body is gripped by a strong force and I'm propelled into what feels like another dimension. I'm instantly surrounded by bright glowing clouds and tendrils of fog and mist. It's incredibly beautiful and very expansive, stretching for hundreds of miles in every direction. The feeling of peace is exquisite and pure.

I am floating along at a pretty fast pace, but this place is so unbelievably vast that it seems like I'm making very little forward progress. This is taking way too long. I know from experience that my ability to remain conscious while out of body for long periods is limited, so I impatiently shout out, "Faster!"

I feel a surge of increased forward motion. I'm passing through tendrils of mist and past giant clouds, but still I don't see anything resembling the *Titanic*. I keep flying for a few more minutes, but again I become impatient. This is taking way too long.

I look down below me. It's a thick layer of white, glowing mists. I'm becoming more impatient and I begin to wonder what's below all those clouds. I just can't wait another second. I dive straight down through them.

I suddenly pop through the clouds. Below me is a vast tropical wilderness. I see lots of lush foliage, trees, rivers. I swoop down low and I'm whizzing past what looks like palm trees and forests of bamboo. There are lots of fields filled with tall grass and lots of different plants with huge leaves. I'm trying to figure out where this is. Could it be Africa? It's warm and sunny, but there's lots of water. I have the distinct impression that it's in the distant past, but I have no idea when.

I see a small clearing. I swoop down and land lightly on my feet. I'm studying the plant life to see if I can determine where I am. Suddenly my attention is diverted to movement in front of me.

About twenty feet in front of me is a very large lioness. The color of her fur matches the color of the dry grass perfectly. I didn't see her until she stood up on her haunches. She now pushes her paws forward, puts her head down, and hunches her back. I recognize the posture; she is about to attack. I scream out "Lion!!"

Before I can do anything, the lion pounces at me. Its jaws are instantly around my throat. Even though I know this is a dream lion, I'm totally freaked out. Taken by surprise, I panic and fly away as fast as I can. Seconds later, I lose consciousness. (July 19, 1997)

Many advanced astral travelers have written that they were able to discover their past lives while out of body. Robert Monroe, Bruce Moen, Marilyn Hughes, and others have done this, so I figured I would give it a try.

I already had some indication of past lives in the form of powerful dreams. In one dream, I was a black man during slave times. In the dream I was held prisoner in a wealthy Southern mansion for some minor infraction. I escaped because an old white lady in a wheelchair helped me to escape. I was reunited with my family. I will never forget the gratitude I felt for that old white lady and the love I felt for my black mother.

In another dream, I was a victim of the Jewish holocaust. I was taken to a concentration camp. In the dream, we were kept running at all times. We were run up to a large pit. One by one, we were shot in the back and fell into the pit filled with bodies.

In a third dream, I was a young Native American boy during colonial times. I went on some sort of manhood ritual with two other boys. We were led by our teacher/guide to a remote, unknown location in the wilderness, where we were abandoned. We had to perform three tasks. The first was to find our way back from where we were abandoned. The second was to track our teacher. The third was to climb a cliff while wearing a backpack filled with stones. That was the hardest of all three tasks and caused me considerable fear. I was the second to climb. I will never forget the comradeship I felt with my fellow students, and especially the love, respect, and awe for my teacher.

But these were all just dreams. I was eager to *consciously* explore any past life memories. As is usually the case, I was shocked at what actually happened.

A Past Life

I'm lucid. I fly out of my body and, pop! I'm at my father's house. Everything looks pristine and realistic. I fly through the house to try to get over my excitement at being out of body. Once I get it out of my system, I think about doing an experiment.

I shout out, "I want to see my past life!" Suddenly I am pulled off the ground and forward. Everything around me looks normal except I see some kind of barrier ahead of me. It looks almost like a huge, flat TV screen with a lifelike scene coming directly at me. I only have a brief second to watch as the scene crashes over me, engulfs me, and pulls me inside of it.

There's a shift and I'm not only in another place and time; I am another person. I am a young woman, about 25 years old. I am wearing a tight knee-length skirt and a thin blouse. I am walking down the side of a rural road at night. There are no sidewalks or streetlights. I'm on my way home.

A car approaches down the road. I can only see the head-lights, and as it gets close, I appear in the headlights and the car immediately slows down. It is obvious the driver sees me. I become nervous; all my instincts are crying out: Danger!

The car is coming to a stop about twenty feet ahead of me. I shield my eyes. I am trying to see who it is. At the same time, I feel like a deer caught in the headlights. I just don't feel safe at all. I feel so vulnerable.

While all this is happening, I'm trying to think, "Where am I? When is this?" I'm trying to determine the make and model of the car to narrow down the date. All of this is rushing through my mind, while simultaneously I'm becoming increasingly apprehensive about what is going to happen.

The car stops and the door opens. I see a man's figure step out and move towards me. Instantly, the memory of what happened (is going to happen) floods into me. The man is going to attack me. I'm about to be raped and killed. I am certain of it. I know what is going to happen, and I really do not want to experience it again.

I start shaking my head back and forth to end the experience and wake myself up. It works, and I am back in bed. (September 30, 1997)

I call this next experience a high-level OBE because I had the distinct impression that I had entered a finer dimension. For the first time, I was getting some real control.

Another Dimension

I see my mother, and realizing she is dead, become lucid. Because she is a projection, she disappears. My father's house coalesces around me. Determined to erase all illusion, I spin around as fast as I can go. The house dissolves in a swirl of color and movement.

I find myself hurtling upwards at very high speed. At first I see blue sky, but there's a shift.

Suddenly, everything around me is very bright. I've been here before. This is the foggy dimension. Around me stretching for hundreds of miles is this vast space with beautiful glowing clouds, mists, and tendrils of fog. I am just the tiniest floating speck in an expansive dimension. Fantastic formations of clouds are above and below me and on all sides. It is so beautiful here.

I am moving forward at what feels like a slow rate, but I reason it must be faster than it seems because I am such a small dot in an endless sea of fog and clouds. I am very patient and waiting for my destination to appear.

Suddenly, I feel a strange shift, as if I am passing through a barrier. I feel a sharp increase of lucidity, and am instantly aware that I am in an upper dimension. I'm thinking of all the planes as they are described in Eastern religions. I wonder, is this the Akashic plane, the Causal plane, the Buddhic plane, or what? I don't know enough about it to say. But I do know one thing: Whatever thoughts I have will be instantly manifested and the fact that nothing is appearing around me means that I am not having thoughts, which means that I've taken another step in controlling my OBEs.

I look around me. Everything is very bright, but now it looks and feels more crystalline, more pure. It almost feels like I am embedded in super-clear crystal, only everything is very smooth and clear and free. It feels great.

I am amazed to be here and am very careful to guard my thoughts. To keep my mind occupied and to maintain my awareness, I use the running commentary technique. I repeat, "I am dreaming! I am dreaming! I am dreaming!"

Ironically, I know this is not really a dream at all, but this device works well to keep my mind busy. I am determined not to let my thoughts run wild as I am convinced they will manifest instantly.

Finally, I decide it's time to gather my courage and at least try to manifest something.

I start with small objects like clocks, pens, tables, chairs, and other objects. After I create them, I examine them carefully. They look totally real. To further test them, I fly through the objects. I can't feel them at all.

Feeling brave, I decide to create people. Boom! People appear around me. I have no idea who they are, but I am certain they are my projections. I am amazed at how lifelike they seem to be.

I'm getting the feeling that I've been here many times before. In some ways, it reminds me of the crystal dimension where I visited my mother. Remembering how good the orange crystals tasted, I decide to manifest a tall, cool glass of fresh-squeezed orange juice.

Instantly, a glass of orange juice is in my hand. It is a little shorter than I expected and reminds me of restaurant-served orange juice. I lift the glass up and drink it down. The orange juice flows across my tongue and down my throat like living nectar. It tastes *so* good and *so* orange. This is great, and I'm loving it. At this point, my memory fails me, other than I recall doing other experiments and going somewhere else. (November 1, 1997)

In the following experience I made another visit to the Heavenly Realms or perhaps "The Park," as Robert Monroe designated it. Honestly, I don't know for sure, but it was one of my more profound OBEs.

The Park

I'm lying in bed when I feel the vibrations. I allow them to grow until they become very strong. Suddenly, I can't feel my physical body. There's a strong whooshing sensation, and I'm out. I can't see anything. It takes me a few moments to get my astral sight. I'm shaking my head and trying to focus, trying to raise my awareness. After a lot of effort, I manage to see a few lights and shadows. It slowly clears up and, no surprise, I'm at Dad's house.

I fly outside. It's dark and quiet. I know for a fact that my body is about ten miles away asleep in bed and that I'm out of body. I fly outside and around the house, up to the driveway. I see some dogs and try to interact. I don't know if they're real, but they seem to see me. I call out, "Clarity! More awareness!"

I feel a strong increase in consciousness. I fly up and around. I love flying while out of body. I think about my body in bed, and for some strange reason, I wonder if it can physically levitate. I keep flying, up and up.

Suddenly, I feel something grab my ankle. It feels like a small hand. Is this one of those lower astral life forms I've read about? I wonder. It is definitely slowing me down. I reach down and easily pry the fingers off. I fly away and upwards until there's a shift.

I pop out in another place. I'm walking down a thin pathway winding through a small, green valley filled with rolling hills. Other small groups of people are passing back and forth along the pathways. Everything is bright and cheery. I recognize this place. It's The Park, the Heavenly Realms. I've been here before. It's a very nice place and I feel great.

I'm overly excited and out of focus. I try to run up to people, but I can't seem to reach them. Nobody sees me. I finally reach out and grab somebody by the shoulders and say, "Who are you?"

The person turns his head, avoids my gaze, and walks away. I become frustrated at my inability to evoke a response, so I call out, "I want to see God!"

Nothing happens, so I call out, "I want to see my Higher Self!"

Nothing happens. I can feel that I'm reaching the end of my rope of awareness so I decide to move on. I jump up and fly away at incredible speeds.

There's a shift and I'm in a lower dimension. I recognize this place too. This is one of the thought-responsive realms. I create a television and turn it on. I see a vivid desert scene, which looks like the southwestern United States. There's no sound, so I fiddle with the volume knob. To my delight, I can make the sound go loud or soft. This is the first time I've been able to control volume. I am delighted at this new ability and play with it for a few minutes until I wake up. (April 21, 2002)

Many OBE travelers report what is known as a "rescue" or a "soul-retrieval." Apparently, in some cases after people die, they do not realize that they are dead. For various reasons, they remain attached to the physical dimension and their deceased loved ones are unable to reach them.

In these cases, living astral travelers can assist in moving the lost soul on to the next dimension. Many OBEers find themselves doing this whether they want to or not. In some cases, it appears that they are rescuing the souls of their own past lives.

After rereading some of the OBE literature, I realized that I had never had this experience. So I decided that it would be my next experiment. I spent the evening before bed in meditation on this concept and then went to bed with the intent on my mind. I was, as usual, amazed by the result.

Soul Retrieval

I'm lucid. Looking around me, I'm at Dad's house. I try to fly through the wall, but I bounce off. I pick another wall and fly through it. I pop out the other side. I'm in the backyard. I am out of body. I fly up to the top of the eucalyptus tree. I fly around the tops of other trees, grabbing the leaves, trying to pick them and smell them. I can't smell anything.

I have some memory lapse here. I think I remembered my plan to go visit David and then Roger. I think I went to see them, but I can't quite remember.

The next thing I remember is my desire to participate in a rescue/retrieval of a person who doesn't know that he or she has died. I state the desire and I feel a sudden, powerful force grab my astral body and propel it upwards.

There's a shift, and suddenly I'm in a different dimension. I can't see anything. It's totally black. I have no idea where I am, but I'm paying careful attention to what might happen next. After a few moments, I see a little girl, about five years old. She's Caucasian, has long blond hair, and is wearing nice clothes. She reminds me of the small girl in the movie *Poltergeist*. I see nothing else around her. She's just standing there, looking a little sad and confused.

I love children, and as soon as I see her, I rush up to her and say, "Oh, my poor child." I open my arms and hug her tightly. She hugs me back, whimpering slightly. She seems too tired to cry. I say, "Poor dear, come here," and hold her.

Although normally very emotional, especially while out of body, I am able to keep my emotions in check. I have no idea who this girl is, or what happened to her. (A vague impression here of suffocation? Stuck underneath a house?) But I know that I love her and must help her.

Acting as an authority figure, I tell her, "Okay, let's go," and I grab her hand.

At this point, I can't see her except in my mind's eye, and the image is hard to hold onto. So I grip her hand tightly and we fly upwards. I'm thinking how amazing this is. I remember accounts of retrievals done by Robert Monroe and Bruce Moen. Both wrote that on occasion they had difficulty tracking what happened to the people they helped. Suddenly they would just disappear. For this reason, I'm paying very careful attention to the feeling of the girl's hand in mine, making sure that she doesn't disappear on me.

We're moving quickly forward or upward. I'm focusing my attention on getting to the heavenly realms. I can't see anything but I get the impression that we're getting close or that we are already there.

I don't know who is here to meet the girl, but instinctively I know she wants to see her mother. I say, "Are you ready to see your Mommy?"

At that exact instant, I feel her release my hand or she just disappears. I get no sense of where she went. There's a shift and I'm back in the darkness where I originally found her. I am very excited and am anxious about possibly forgetting what just happened. I know from experience that I've forgotten many, many, many experiences.

There's a point of light ahead of me. I focus on it, and it expands into a scene. I'm in a small space, which reminds me of a crawlspace or someplace underground. It's dark except for a few feet in front me. I see a pile of treasure! There is a large pile of different-sized gold coins lying half-buried in the soil.

I know instantly that these coins represent my memories of this experience. Looking at the HUGE pile, I also know that there is no way I'm going to be able to carry it all back with me. Only slightly sad about this (I'm so grateful to be where I am), I act quickly. I start scooping up the coins. I go for the big ones, thinking that they represent the big events, but just for good measure, I scoop up a few small ones too. I grab as many as I can and clutch them to my chest. I carry them out into the light.

There's a shift and I wake up amazed. (July 15, 2002)

Although I did lose some memory of this event, I was still very pleased with the outcome.

Another goal was to make contact with my spirit guide. I had already had some contact of this kind. There was the black lady who pushed me through the wall. There were the man and the woman who sang to me (this happened a few times). I had tried several times to make contact by shouting out, "Show me my spirit guides!" or, "I want to contact a highly evolved being." This had not worked for me.

Then I read in one of Bruce Moen's books that if you haven't made contact with your spirit guide, try looking behind you during your OBE and you may be surprised to find somebody there, guiding you. Many projectors, including Wilson, Moen, and Monroe, have apparently seen arms or faces or entire figures encouraging them or, more commonly, guiding their astral journeys. I couldn't wait to try this.

I Contact a Spirit Guide

I wake up early in the morning. Feeling very relaxed, I try to have an OBE. I'm lying on my stomach, drifting deeper and deeper. I'm just at the point before sleep when I feel my legs floating upwards. For a second, I think I'm physically levitating, but I quickly realize what is happening. I'm halfway out of body. I marvel at the strange sensation, as I do not usually exit this direction: backwards, legs first. The top half of my astral body is still attached to the physical, and I'm kicking my astral legs around like a bug stuck in the mud. When that doesn't work, I easily take my astral arms and do an astral push-up right out of my body.

I'm floating about one foot above my body, perfectly parallel to it. I fly up and look around. I'm at my dad's house. I fly through the window. As sometimes happens, I have a little trouble and have to tear my way through the window.

I pop out on the outside of the house. Everything looks totally real, but I just don't know. I fly down to the street and look around. I decide to try to contact Christy. I shout out, "Christy! Christy!" At first my voice cracks and barely works, but after a couple of tries, I call her name strongly.

I feel a slight tug, and I'm floating lazily down the street at about three miles per hour. At this rate, it will take me hours to get to her house. Then I remember another thing I wanted to try, which was to contact my spirit guide.

Remembering the advice to look behind me, I stop, whirl 180 degrees, and look behind me.

At first I see nothing but the road and trees on either side. But then I see a small coyote dart very quickly across the road diagonally from right to left. I think it was a coyote. Maybe it was a fox. I keep looking and I see it dart across the road again, this time from left to right. It is creeping very low to the ground and is obviously stalking me.

I am amused and intensely curious. I was expecting a person, not an animal. I get a vague feeling of mischief, love, and a sort of distant pride emanating from the coyote. If this is my spirit guide, he is a definite trickster—I'm thinking probably a Native American shaman (I've always felt a connection to this subject). I feel a definite sense of company from the coyote.

I turn around and am shocked to see that a bird is flying straight at me. I have no time to duck. It flies right into my face and through my head. The pun "bird brain" comes to mind. I am so shocked I wake up. (August 24, 2002)

Around this time, I became interested in visiting the Akashic plane. I had no idea where it was or what it looked like. From what I had read, the Akashic plane is a library that records every single event in absolute detail. It allegedly contains not only the past, but future events. I wasn't sure what I wanted to research, but I knew that this would be an interesting place to visit. On my first attempt, I didn't quite make it.

In Search of the Akashic Library

I am lucid. I induce the vibrations and roll easily out of my body. I see nothing but total blackness. Suddenly, I'm surrounded by tiny white dots of light that slowly coalesce into a scene. I'm flying over the nearby Santa Monica Mountains. A dark tunnel opens in front of me and, as it obviously appeared for my benefit, I enter it. As I fly through the tunnel, I examine it closely. The lighting is very dim, but I can make out rock walls. I see a mirror and examine my reflection. I feel a boost of excitement to be out of body. I am really wondering where this tunnel is leading.

Suddenly, there's an opening and I easily pop out of it. I'm on a train filled with passengers moving through the countryside! Slightly disoriented, I look around me. Everyone seems dressed strangely, as if this were the 1800s. It's moving along briskly. Slightly alarmed and wondering if I popped out of the tunnel too soon, I fly out of the train. There's another shift.

I'm in a beautiful park. There's my sister Valerie and her son. I am amazed to see them. Suddenly, I begin to lose consciousness and am able to maintain it by fixing my gaze on various objects. I take off and I start flying, flying, flying to I-don't-know-where. I shout out, "Take me to the Akashic Plane!"

I keep flying until I pop out in a very bright area. I'm having trouble maintaining focus, but I can see I'm in a natural-looking setting with trees, fields, and flowers. It's very, very bright; everything is literally glowing with white light. Several hundred yards to my right, I see a stone or marble building. It is a large Roman-looking structure with huge white pillars in front. I feel a strong pull towards it, and get a strong impression that it is the Akashic Library. I gulp and wonder if I could possibly be worthy of entering that magnificent structure.

I am too nervous, so I take off flying. Suddenly, I see my sister Victoria. She says she has a pain in her left side. I heal her by sticking my astral hands inside her at the area of the discomfort.

Afterwards, I see another tunnel. I feel the compulsion to dive into it. In seconds, I pop out on the other side. I'm in bright, beautiful sunshine. To my amazement, I can actually feel

the warmth of the sunlight on my body. It feels great! I'm loving this, but I have no idea at all where I am. I get the feeling
that this is the physical world. I see cars. Am I over the freeway
north of my home?

As if on cue, I suddenly hear sounds in my condo, normal
traffic noises, or people in the hallway. I'm being pulled back.
In an instant I'm back in my bedroom and back in my body.
(October 5, 2002)

While I didn't quite make it to the Akashic Library, I wasn't
about to give up. I thought that maybe I needed to increase my
vibrations, so next time I was out of body, I shouted out, "Raise my
vibration!" To my amusement, my astral body was propelled
upwards, but otherwise nothing happened. In another OBE
episode, I shouted out, "I want to see an advanced being!" I was
hoping someone would show up and take me to the library, but
nothing happened.

When I finally actually made it to the Akashic Library, I could
not have been happier and the experience turned out to be one
of the most profound of my life.

Inside the Akashic Library

I'm lucid. I slide sideways out of my body and off the bed.
I fly upwards into space and start calling out "Mom! Mom!
Mom!" I fly in a wandering path as I keep calling out, "Mom"
over and over again. She almost never shows up when I call
her—our visits are always on her terms, not mine—but this
time, I'm not giving up. I keep calling her, picturing her, reaching out to her. I call her twenty times, forty times. I'm flying
around and can see nothing but white space. Then to my utter
amazement and delight, my mother pops in front of me! We
rush up and hug. The feeling of reunion is intense. She has
been so patient with me bugging her like this. I can't believe
how beautiful she looks and how great it is to see her. We talk
for a while. I can't seem to remember most of the conversation.

I remember finally telling her I wanted to see the Akashic

Library. She takes me by the hand and leads me outside. For the first time, I realize we are inside a room. She tells me I must go on alone. I start flying upwards. There's a shift, and I'm suddenly inside the Akashic Library.

I'm in a small room. The floors, walls, and ceiling are made of glowing quartz crystal, or sparkly white marble. Everything is glowing white and dazzling with unbelievable beauty. The room is rectangular. I think there's someone behind me, directing me. There's an open doorway and a hallway. But I'm too amazed by what's on the walls to pay attention to what's behind me. A bunch of what look like mirrors or screens are placed around the walls. I'm so amazed that I lift my left arm up and stare at it to see if it will disappear. This will verify that I am actually out of body. Sure enough, my arm dissolves, starting with the fingers and going downwards.

I turn away and gaze deeply into one of the screens. I see all my past lives whiz past in quick succession. The speed is intense; it's like flipping through a deck of cards, way too fast for me to retain any detail. The message is clear. Although I'm not given any details at all about my past lives, I now know that there have been many.

The images flit by, one after another, and then suddenly stop on one particular image. To my amazement, this is not a past life, but a future life! At least, that's the impression I get. In the screen I see the three-dimensional image of a handsome man. He is bald and has the most amazing silver eyes. He seems ageless and incredibly wise and loving. I'm wondering if he's even from this planet. Although he looks human, his eyes are so mesmerizing. Suddenly, I'm not sure if he's just an image or if I'm actually meeting him. Did we exchange words? Do I remember kneeling in front of him and asking questions? I'm so emotionally moved I can't retain awareness and wake up some time later. (November 19, 2002)

About two months later, I managed to make another foray to the Akashic Library.

The Akashic Library

I'm lucid. I fly upwards and upwards until everything becomes dark and I hit a massive barrier. This is the veil between the dimensions. It feels like a solid wall stretching forever in all directions. All I know is I want to get to the other side. I start pounding and clawing at the barrier, trying to get through. The song "Knocking on Heaven's Door" comes to my mind as I try to rip my way into the next dimension. Finally, I rip open a tiny hole. Instantly, the hole floods forth with beautiful, divine, heavenly light. I rip it open and climb/squirm my way through the hole into a dimension of pure light. Everything ugly in me is left behind, as if the veil is like a screen that sifts out all the unwanted psychological baggage. I'm now standing in a beautiful nature scene, light and airy and very bright. I'm on a small, grassy hill overlooking a beautiful blue lake. The water is shimmering and glinting like a thousand diamonds. The hills and trees are glowing so brightly, it almost overwhelms the colors. I feel calm, peaceful, and pure.

I fly upwards, and beyond the lake in the distance I see the Akashic Library. Flying or looking closer, I can see it clearly. It stands several stories tall and has maybe a dozen tall white pillars in front. The architecture reminds me of the United States Capital Building, only it's larger and more exquisite. I am totally fascinated by its appearance.

The scene shifts and I am back in my bedroom. I plop back in my body. Still feeling the vibrations, I swoop out and float outside onto my balcony. It's still dark out. Suddenly, I swoop into another person's apartment in my building and observe him sleeping in bed. I didn't mean to do it and can't control myself. I know it stems from an earlier unexpressed desire to see who lived in this particular unit. After I observe him, I return and wake up. (January 25, 2003)

Although I had experienced many visits to the "Other Side," I still had many questions about what it was like to live in the afterlife. My next experience taught me well what's it like to just relax and enjoy yourself on the astral plane.

Relaxing on an Astral Beach

I'm lucid. Looking around me, I am delighted to see that I am out of body and in the heavenly realms. I'm on an astral beach. I know that I am here to just relax, enjoy myself, and observe life on the astral plane. There are several people around relaxing on the beach, watching the ocean. I lie there, soaking in the energy of the place, relieved to finally be here. I always feel a strong sense of relief when I'm here.

I become fascinated by the ocean. The water is so blue and pure. It moves differently. The water seems lighter; the waves are huge, but gentler, as if perfectly designed for body surfing. I see people in the water swimming. I dive into the water and am amazed by its texture. While I can feel the water, it's almost like I have a bubble of air around me. There's a smoothness to the sensation that's difficult to describe. I can stay underwater as long as I want. I swim up to a wave and it carries me very high. The feeling of movement is very pronounced and is very much like body surfing in real life, only more dramatic. I ride the waves like a roller coaster for a few more minutes, then return to the beach. I lie there in meditation, then wake up. (April 19, 2003)

11

OBEs and Psychic Powers

Learning out-of-body travel is interesting, fun, and exciting. However, there are certain consequences. Once you get good at projecting, you may find that the experience begins to invade your waking life.

While I haven't experienced anything bad, or even scary, I kept confronting bizarre situations. Nobody warned me that integrating the dream state with your waking consciousness would lead to possible confusion and a bleed-through between the physical and astral dimensions.

Over and over again, dreams and reality would merge until they were sometimes indistinguishable. I found it necessary to be extremely cautious and observant of my surroundings because at times telling the difference between a dream and reality became problematic.

As memories poured into my mind throughout the day, it was sometimes difficult to differentiate which were dream memories and which were waking memories. Both were equally vivid and realistic.

The most startling consequence, however, was precognition. After virtually every lucid episode, I would have precognitive dreams. This is apparently not uncommon. Writes Muldoon, "In fact, scarcely a week goes by without some future-contemplating dream . . ." (Muldoon and Carrington 1929, 1973, p. 301).

Many other projectors have also experienced a sudden flood of psychic experiences, including Patricia Garfield, Robert Monroe, Robert Peterson, Bruce Moen, Robert Bruce, Albert Taylor, and others. Apparently this is a pretty consistent side effect of OBE travel.

Although several of the books warned about this, I started having OBEs before many of them were published. And those that did warn me didn't really explain just how much OBEs can change your waking perception and awareness.

When you start having dreams that actually play out in front of you in the physical life, it becomes clear that your dreams are actually the "real world" and that physical reality is a dream. It can get very confusing.

Writes Robert Peterson, "I had asked for out-of-body experiences, not psychic experiences. Somehow I had gotten them both. Somehow I was becoming psychic, whether I wanted it or not. I absolutely loved the psychic things that were starting to happen, but I started to worry about my sanity. . . . As a skeptic, I didn't want to believe in psychic experiences. I thought it was all a load of rubbish. But in the years ahead, as I kept practicing OBEs, I also kept having psychic experiences. Most days I would have three to five experiences I would classify as 'psychic'" (Peterson 1997, p. 65).

This transformation was very dramatic for me too. My perception and awareness of the world completely changed. This aspect of my experiences was so overwhelming that it would take another book to fully explore. However, I would like to cover a few experiences here.

I remember one occasion where the experience was particularly frightening.

"Preston, Wake Up!"

My sister Victoria wins first place in a Christmas tree decorating contest. She receives a beautiful gold metal ribbon with engravings on it. I can see the words, but for some reason, I can't make out what it says.

In my confusion, the dream shifts. I'm in my bedroom at night, and I hear Victoria call my name from directly outside my open window. She is saying over and over, "Preston, wake up!" She is saying it so loud and insistently that I wake up. (December 5, 1990)

I was awake in bed. I knew for sure I was awake, and I knew for sure I was not dreaming or asleep. I marvel at the fact that in my dream, Victoria shouted for me to wake up, and I did.

Then suddenly, I heard something that chilled me to the bone. Right outside my window, I heard Victoria shout, "Preston, wake up!"

I totally freaked out. I knew I was awake. Victoria lived in another city. She absolutely could not be outside my window, period. Thoughts rushed through my head. Someone is out there, but who? It can't be my sister! But I distinctly heard her voice.

I sat up and peered out the window, when I heard her again. "Preston, wake up!" My heart thumped in my chest. Was this her ghost?

She called again, "Preston, wake *ruff! Preston, ruff, ruff! Ruff, ruff, ruff! Ruff, ruff, ruff!*"

I realized with shock that it was not my sister I was hearing at all. It was the neighbor's dog barking. Somehow, I had incorporated the sound into my dream, translating into something I could understand, which was my sister saying, "Preston, wake up!"

But when I really did wake up, I still heard my sister's voice. It was as if I was still in the dream state when I was actually awake. I was awake, and yet the dream was still happening. It was a very strange type of bleed-through.

On another occasion, I experienced this effect more dramatically. I was dreaming that somebody was caressing my genitals. The sensation was incredibly erotic and so powerful, it woke me up. However, as I lay there awake in bed, I continued to feel the sensation of being caressed. It felt exactly as if an invisible person was trying to make love to me. Anybody not familiar with the phenomenon would surely believe they were being molested by a ghost. I was more fascinated than scared. After a few seconds, it stopped.

The most bizarre effect from OBE travel, however, was a sudden and dramatic emergence of psychic and paranormal events. Every time I increased my abilities to become lucid and go out of body, I noticed a corresponding increase in psychic abilities.

With one minor exception, I had never displayed any psychic abilities growing up. However, shortly after I started going out of body, I began to have precognitive dreams. These soon turned into waking visions. More and more, lucidity began to occur in the waking world, and I would find myself filled with a strong, sudden, knowing feeling.

For example, on the morning of April 18, 1992, I woke up with a powerful impulse to run out onto my balcony. Even though it was still predawn and I had hours to sleep before I was supposed to get up, the impulse was too strong to resist.

So before I really even knew what I was doing, I walked out onto my balcony. I stood there only for a few seconds, wondering what I was doing standing out there in my underwear. Suddenly, within ten seconds, an earthquake struck.

I watched in morbid fascination as transformers began exploding in showers of sparks. The building shook violently, and car alarms for miles around began blaring. The shaking continued for about fifteen seconds. It felt like a large earthquake, at least five points on the Richter scale.

After the shaking stopped, I ran back inside and switched on the television to see if there was any information.

None of the news stations had any information, so after about ten minutes, I turned the television off. It was still early, and I was still tired, so, marveling at the incredible coincidence of waking up before an earthquake happened, and wondering just how big it was, I went back to sleep. Then I had the following dream.

Boulders on the Road

I am flying over a large mountain range. The geography is typical of Southern California. I swoop lower and see a long, winding mountain road. I am shocked to see that there are large boulders all over the road. I see many cars inching along the highway. They have to swerve all over the road to get past the boulders. (April 8, 1992)

I woke up from the dream and looked at my alarm clock. It was still more than an hour before I had to get up, and I was annoyed. Then, for some unknown reason, I felt compelled to go out onto my balcony again. And again, I wondered, "What the heck am I doing?"

Boom! Another earthquake hit. It was just like the first one— brief and strong, rumbling across the valley, setting off car alarms.

This time, I was truly shocked. The first time could have been a coincidence, but this was crazy! I had been in many earthquakes in the past, and never before did I wake up before they hit, not to mention going onto my balcony in my underwear!

I ran inside and turned on the television. To my amazement, there was my dream. A news helicopter was hovering over a mountain road that was blocked by huge boulders. Cars were lined up, inching down the road, swerving around the boulders. It was my dream exactly.

The news went on to say that it was a double earthquake centered near Big Bear, California, measuring 6.5 on the Richter scale.

A final endnote to the experience. I went to the office and one of my co-workers reported that she was actually in Big Bear on the night of the earthquake. She was unaccountably anxious and hadn't been able to sleep all night, which was totally out of character for her. When the earthquake finally hit, she knew that it was the reason for all her anxiety. As they left Big Bear, they were in one of the cars that was forced to spend hours inching along the highway, avoiding countless giant boulders all over the road.

That is just one example from hundreds. I have had precognitive dreams that predicted illness, death, gifts, unexpected visits, and numerous trivial events. Before long, these precognitive dreams became waking visions. I was plunged headfirst into the world of clairvoyance, clairaudience, clairsentience, precognition, and many other psychic phenomena. A word of advice to would-be astral travelers—be prepared for changes in your perception in the waking world.

12

How to Have OBEs and What to Do When You Succeed

There are many different ways to get out of your body. Most methods include total relaxation of both body and mind, and then either visualizations, affirmations, or some type of exercise. The literature on this is extensive and the would-be astral traveler is strongly encouraged to fully research methods from each author.

Step One: Getting Out

I have refined the following three steps to get out of body.

1. Lie down and relax your body to the point that your body begins to feel sensations of heaviness, lightness, numbness, vertigo, or vibrations. If you don't feel one or more of these sensations, you are not relaxed enough. After this point you are nearly ready for liftoff. For me this usually takes about twenty

minutes of absolutely no movement. You should be able to relax to the point that you cannot feel your body.

2. As you relax your body, allow the thoughts in your mind to become quiet. We all have a constant mind chatter. Turn your attention inward, away from your body and to your thoughts. Allow them to pass and become quiet. You want to get to the point where you are just about to fall asleep and the thoughts in your mind turn into images.

3. Visualize, imagine, intend, desire, and remember to go out of body. See yourself existing outside your body. Imagine your astral body leaving your physical body. Firmly set your intention to have an OBE. Tell yourself, "I will go out of body."

Those are the three main steps. Once you master the relaxation and concentration necessary to launch an OBE, you can use one of the following methods to initiate your OBE. That's all it really takes. After about three tries, you should definitely begin to get results. Please be patient if you don't go immediately out of your body. Just relax and keep trying.

Vibrations. Relax until you feel your body become heavy or start buzzing. When you start to feel the buzzing, relax and increase the vibrations or allow the vibrations to increase until they reach a threshold that propels you out of your body.

Running. Imagine or visualize yourself running as fast as you can. If you are sufficiently relaxed you will run right out of your body.

Spinning. Imagine yourself spinning. This will move your astral body out of phase with your physical body and propel you out of body.

Boat. Imagine yourself sitting on the bow of a boat in the waves, moving up and down. If you are sufficiently relaxed, this will lift you out of your body.

Rope. Visualize a rope hanging above you. Imagine yourself climbing up it, pulling yourself up out of your body.

Rolling Out. Imagine yourself rocking back and forth and just rolling, stepping, or falling out of bed. This is probably the most common method used by projectors.

Elevator. Visualize yourself stepping into an elevator and traveling upwards. This will lift you up out of your body.

Cliff. Visualize a cliff and see yourself standing at its edge and jumping off. This will take you right out.

Lucid Dream Projection. Throughout your waking day, seriously ask yourself if you are dreaming right now. Look around you to see if there are any anomalies. At night, you will ask this same question in the dream state. As you look around your dream environment, you will see anomalies. You will then wake up to the fact that you are dreaming, while you are dreaming. At that point, you are already out of body.

The most important thing to remember about OBEs is to remember them. This cannot be overstated. The fact is, we all have OBEs every night, but we do not remember. We are all in a state of profound amnesia. Otherwise, we would remember all our past lives and all our dreams.

Therefore, the real trick to having OBEs is a good memory. Dream recall is paramount, as many dreams are actually half-remembered OBEs. Each morning, immediately after you wake, do not move. Lie still and try to remember what you were doing, where you were, and who you were with. This will often bring back memories of your dreams and OBEs.

Below is an account of how I used the running method to go out of body. The nickname for this method is "The Flash." While lying down totally relaxed, you pretend that you are running like the super hero The Flash.

The Flash

I am lucid. I remember the method of running like The Flash to propel yourself out of body. I start running with all my might. With a whoosh, I find myself out of body. I am running down a rainy street late at night. I reach a large, dark wall. I jump up into it, and promptly lose consciousness. (March 26, 1995)

The Flash

I'm lucid. I imagine myself running as fast as I can. It works great. I feel a whoosh and I'm running down a street. Strangely, I can't seem to move my right arm at all. I see a man, and start running after him. He turns around and confronts me. I run up to him and try to knock him down. He easily dodges me. (May 2, 1995)

As you progress, you will find that are able to project consciously, without ever losing awareness.

Step Two: Control

Now that you know how to get out of body, the next step is what to do once you get there. If you're like most people, you will be confronted with a few obstacles.

Controlling Emotions. The first few times, you may find yourself overcome with powerful emotions, usually fear or excitement. It's one thing to talk about going out of your body, but it's quite another when you actually find yourself there. The best advice is to meditate while out of body. Keep calm and allow your analytical mind to remain dominant. Try to control your emotions. I got over the fear barrier after only a few scary projections, but it took me years before I was able to gain some measure of control over my excitement. Each person is different. Just be prepared for emotional hurricanes.

Maintaining Awareness. Once you get out of body, you may find it very difficult to stay awake. You may find you have memory problems or cannot think clearly. To maintain awareness, try physically spinning. Try shouting out, "More awareness!" or "Increase lucidity!" Another good trick is to keep what Robert Bruce calls a "running commentary." Tell yourself over and over that you are out of body, and commit to memory exactly what you are seeing and doing. I learned this trick early on, and it does wonders for maintaining your consciousness and memory.

Learning to See. Novice projectors may find that once they get out of body, they are partially or totally blind. To improve your ability to see, I suggest Buhlman's advice to shout out, "Clarity!" Try shaking your head or very slowly opening and closing your eyes. Try peering around you, looking for a spot of light. Then focus on that until it expands into a scene. Try visualizing or imagining images in your mind's eye. Spinning may also work.

Learning Movement. A novice projector might suddenly find herself floating in the middle of her room with no idea how to move. This is one of the funniest parts of learning OBE travel. Learning to fly and walk through walls can present a great challenge. The trick is practice. Instead of trying to walk or run, simply look at the destination you want to reach and will yourself there. Try leaping up and flying. To move through objects, you can go fast or slow. Simply gather your courage and walk through a wall. The sensation is incredible. If you bounce off, remind yourself that you are out of body, that nothing can hurt you, and try again. To visit a person, shout out their name or visualize them or simply fly to them.

That's all there is to it.

Now that you know how to initiate an OBE and now that you have the tools to maintain the fragile state of consciousness, you are ready to do some exploring.

The possibilities are literally infinite. The astral planes are so vast that they have only been partially explored, especially by conscious, living projectors.

Here are some things you might want to try.

Explore the Physical World. Fly around your home or maybe travel to a friend's house. This will get you used to the feeling of being out of body, and give you the experience you need for further adventures.

Visiting the Deceased. Choose somebody you know very well who is deceased. When you are out of body, picture him in your mind, call out his name and ask to visit him. This will be easiest if you pick somebody with whom you have a strong love connection.

Say Your Name. Saying your name while out of body is a fun experiment because you never know what is going to happen.

Ask to See God or Your Higher Self. When you are out of body, call out "I want to see God" or "I want to see my Higher Self." This can initiate some very profound experiences.

The Desire Body. When you are out of body in the astral realms, your thoughts manifest in crystal clarity around you. You can create anything merely by thinking about it. So if you want to have a great feast of food, it is simple to create by simply visualizing it. Or if you want to make love, just place this intention and see what happens. Any fantasy you have can be created. Your imagination is the limit.

Ask to See Your Past Lives. When you are out of body, call out, "I want to see my past lives." If this experiment works, you will be whisked away to relive a past life. Be prepared, however, as this can sometimes be traumatic.

"*Gaom-Raom-Om-Bour-Bu-Mama-Papa.*" Repeat this mantra while out of body. If you are able to say this while out of body or lucid dreaming, you may be surprised.

"Take Me Where I Need to Go." This is my favorite experiment because it is so unpredictable and is always rewarding. Simply go out of body and shout out, "Take me where I need to go."

There are endless numbers of experiments you can do. You can visit the Akashic Planes. You can travel into the past or view the future. You can visit people and places, you can heal yourself and others, attend secret schools of knowledge, contact your spirit guides, fly through dimensions of pure light and love, and so much more.

The benefits of OBEs are inestimable. Furthermore, if you examine the phenomenon carefully and objectively, it is clear that sooner or later, everyone will be having OBEs.

The fact that we die means that one day, we will all have a permanent out-of-body experience. And as humanity evolves spiritually, more and more people will become conscious projectors. The truth, again, is that we all project every night. Sooner or later, more and more people are going to start remembering.

Conscious astral travel is inevitable.

The development of the ability to travel consciously while out of body follows the same patterns in most people. Male projectors seem to outnumber woman projectors. However, this could simply be because more men have had books published on the subject.

Interestingly, many of the reported projectors are strongly left-brained. Businessmen, computer programmers, engineers, analysts, accountants—these are the types that are having OBEs.

About half of all projectors began having OBEs spontaneously and learned to control them. The other half actively pursued the experience after reading about it. About 70 percent report sleep paralysis. Nearly all report psychic events.

The average out-of-body experience follows a set pattern.

1. Relaxation.
2. Sensations of vibrations, vertigo, heaviness, lightness.
3. Separation.
4. Consciousness is perceived as being separate from the body.
5. Return.

The above scenario depicts a fully conscious projection. Many attempts will involve memories of only a few of the steps. For example, in some of my OBEs, I remember only step four. The development of the talent of astral projection follows four steps.

1. **Novice:** Has experienced 1–10 successful projections and can occasionally induce the pre-OBE state (i.e., vibrations). Has difficulties in the following areas: movement, vision, emotional control, mental clarity.

2. **Intermediate:** Has experienced 10–100 successful projections and can regularly induce an OBE. Is able to control emotions long enough to maintain the OBE state for at least one minute. Is able to use vision and has some control over movement. At this stage, the projector is able to conduct various experiments and explorations.

3. **Advanced:** Has experienced 100–1,000 or more successful projections and can induce the out-of-body experience at will using a variety of methods, including consciously induced OBEs. Has control over vision, movement, mental clarity, and emotions. Can maintain the OBE state for at least one hour. Has achieved a number of goals, including obtaining evidence for OBE veracity, traveling to distant locations, visiting deceased, uncovering past lives, exploring some of the higher dimensions, etc.

4. **Expert:** Spiritually enlightened. Has experienced thousands of successful projections and can induce the out-of-body experience at will, including while awake and functioning. Is in touch with all the subtle bodies and higher dimensions. Displays supernormal powers. Has total control. *Immortal?*

13

Questions and Answers

An experience as unusual as the OBE raises many questions. Below are some of the most commonly asked questions.

Q: What exactly is an out-of-body experience?

A: An out-of-body experience (OBE) occurs when an individual perceives his or her awareness as existing outside of the physical body. During the OBE, the individual has a duplicate body and is able to fly through solid objects, to distant locations, and into other dimensions.

Q: How do you know these are not just dreams?

A: Virtually every advanced projector has obtained personal proof that their experiences are not dreams. While beginning projectors may find that their experiences are dreamlike, as you progress in your ability to control the experience, you are able to obtain evidence that you are not dreaming. This evidence usually comes in the form of verifiable information. For example, you travel out of body to a specific location, and then are able to later visit the area in the physical and confirm certain details.

Q: Is going out of body dangerous in any way?

A: No. No, no, no! Not only are OBEs not dangerous, they occur to everybody every night. There is not a single reported case of anybody being physically harmed by an OBE. It is impossible to be hurt while out of body because you are nonphysical. Nor can you get too far away from your body, or locked out, or possessed. While some people have reported scary experiences, there is very little evidence of any actual danger. On the contrary, the evidence supports the opposite scenario, that OBEs promote health, both spiritual and physical.

Q: Can anybody have out-of-body experiences?

A: Yes, absolutely. There seems to be no pattern in terms of culture, educational level, race, sex, age . . . You do it every night! You don't have to be psychic. You don't have to believe in them. You don't have to be healthy or ill. The only requirement is having the desire, and taking the time and effort.

Q: How long does it take to have an OBE?

A: The majority of people will experience pre-OBE sensations such as vertigo, heaviness, lightness, or vibrations during their first three attempts. It took me only a few tries, and most people I've talked to report the same. It's not unusual to experience an OBE on the first attempt. However, some people may encounter a steep learning curve. It all depends on how much effort you put into it. I have taught several people to have OBEs and am convinced anybody can do it if they persist.

Q: I've tried to do the exercises and I can't get out of my body. What am I doing wrong?

A: If you've tried to go out of body and haven't succeeded, you are not following the steps correctly. The keys are relaxation, awareness, visualization, memory, desire, and intention. Relaxation is the first key. You must relax completely. Second, you must remain aware. Get as close to the sleep state as possible without falling asleep. To get out of body, you must visualize yourself lifting out or visualize yourself already out. Jump out. Feel for the vibrations. Relax, keep your mind clear, and go. Memory is the third key. Tell yourself each night that you will remember everything. Robert Monroe's experiences started as a result of sleep-learning tapes. Memory is vital to the OBE. Desire is also crucial. If you really want it, you will be inspired enough to focus. The final key is intention. If you are truly inspired, you will focus your attention, desire, and will on the subject. The more effort you apply, the greater your success will be.

Q: Does it matter what position your physical body is in?

A: No. Some astral travelers report that lying north to south facilitates their projections. I have found that I can project no matter which way I'm facing or what position I'm in. I've projected lying on my stomach, on my side, and on my back. The main factor seems to be relaxation.

Q: Will I be able to visit anywhere I want to go?

A: Yes and no. If you're good at it, you will be able to explore pretty much like a ghost would. I had a few inadvertent experiences during which my desire body took control and I invaded the privacy of women's showers. Hopefully, however, you won't invade people's privacy on purpose. Yes, you can explore anyplace you want, on Earth and beyond. However, good luck getting there. In other words, it is possible, but easier said than done. Traveling while out of body takes a good deal of practice. You can go to other places if you know them well. Traveling to meet people that you know is easier. But flying around and exploring physical places on earth is extremely tricky. As you practice, you get better. But I have found that the other dimensions hold things of more interest.

Q: Do you wake up tired after a night of conscious astral travel?

A: No, on the contrary, astral travel supplies the projector with tremendous energy and vitality. You wake up feeling incredibly refreshed and in a good mood. You can even be healed of physical illness.

Q: If astral travel is so easy, how come everybody isn't doing it?

A: I can only speculate that there is a combination of factors, including the scarcity of information on how to initiate an OBE, the fear of the unknown, the overwhelming demands of physical life, the lack of sufficient sleep, or a lack of curiosity or interest. For myself, it was skepticism. I simply didn't believe it was possible.

Q: How many people have this ability of conscious out-of-body travel?

A: This is very difficult to answer because the vast majority of projectors keep silent. While novice projectors often feel compelled to share what they have learned, they soon learn that most people don't have an interest in OBEs. According to some studies, most people will report at least one OBE in their lifetime. But the number of regular projectors is undoubtedly much smaller. I would guess that there are probably several thousand people with this ability, but that is pure speculation. I just don't know.

Epilogue

As I look back on my experiences, I am somewhat in awe. How could this have happened to me? I was so skeptical of such things. I can find no real clues that would explain it. One experience does come to mind. I was a teenager in the dentist's office. For the first time, I tried nitrous oxide, or "laughing gas." The doctor put the mask on my face and turned it on. Almost instantly, I felt myself losing consciousness. I felt like I was about to fly out of my body and down a dark tunnel that was forming above me. I clawed at the mask and the dentist pulled it off just in time. I had no idea at the time what was happening, but I felt like I was about to die. Looking back, the sensation was somewhat reminiscent of the launching of an OBE.

Another funny incident comes to mind. Early on, when I developed an interest in OBEs and was just beginning my adventures, my sister-in-law Christy went to see a psychic. The psychic gave considerable verifiable information. During her reading, Christy asked the psychic if she had any impressions about me.

Christy taped the reading and I was quite surprised to hear

what the psychic said. Without hesitation she replied, "Oh, he should try to do out-of-body experiences. He would be very good at it."

We had a good laugh at that one. I certainly wasn't very good at that point.

Today, nearly twenty years of out-of-body experiences has taught me many things. Like most projectors, I learned early on that privacy is an illusion. I learned that the universe is far more vast than I can possibly imagine. I learned that beliefs unsupported by experience can lead to delusion and retard spiritual growth. I learned that thoughts and emotions have far-reaching effects.

I have learned that there is, in fact, life after death. I have learned that we are all connected in intricate ways, and that everybody has out-of-body experiences on a nightly basis—they just don't always remember. But most of all, I have learned that the human organism contains an apparently infinite capacity to grow and learn, and that we all have vast untapped powers that we have only begun to explore.

I have also come to the conclusion that *conscious* out-of-body travel will become increasingly common among the general population. I think it's inevitable. Astral projection is not so much a talent as it is a naturally occurring human condition. As people follow their natural paths of spiritual evolution, it is inevitable that sooner or later their abilities to perform conscious astral travel will be activated. In other words, everyone will eventually be astral traveling whether they want to or not. As Robert Bruce writes, "OBE is way too powerful and meaningful to be accidental. So it seems logical to suggest that conscious OBE may be an important part of the spiritual evolutionary process. As mankind evolves, I believe the OBE factor will steadily become a more profound and meaningful part of life, on the individual as well as on the species-growth level" (Bruce, p. 436).

The benefits of learning astral travel should by now be obvious. I consider my OBEs to be among the most powerful and profound experiences of my life. They have been a source of strength and inspiration. They have been unbelievably exciting and the adventures show no signs of ending.

Currently, when things are going well, I have OBEs about four times a month. I can now induce an OBE on a consistent basis, but the majority of them remain short and I still struggle with control problems. My progress has been slow and many times I've taken one step forward and two steps back. I definitely can't call myself an expert yet, but I'm not going to give up. Once you've tasted the exquisite, pure, sweet ecstasy of the out-of-body experience, you are always drawn back to it.

Recently, I've been concentrating on contacting my spirit guide. I was out of body when I remembered again to look behind me. To my surprise, there was that darn coyote. It moved so fast I couldn't keep my eye on it. I chased it across a field as it darted back and forth. It easily outran me and disappeared.

Another interesting thing happened recently. Normally, when I go out of body, I get no outside help, at least none that I'm aware of. Recently, however, I was inducing the vibrations and getting ready to go out of body when I distinctly felt two small hands grab mine. A young female voice said, "Come," and pulled me out of my body. I was so amazed, I only remember bits and pieces after that.

I still have so much more I want to do. Many out-of-body travelers report seeing a silver cord during their OBEs that attaches their astral body to their physical body. I want to see my silver cord (I've never been able to do that, though I've never remembered to try). I'd also like to visit the Akashic Library again and maybe learn a little bit more about my past lives. And I never get tired of visiting the Heavenly realms. Or maybe I'll just use my favorite command, "Take me where I need to go." That always turns out to be interesting.

Sources and Recommended Reading

Bruce, Robert. *Astral Dynamics*. Charlottesville, Virginia: Hampton Roads Publishing Co, 1999.

Buhlman, William. *Adventures Beyond the Body: How to Experience Out-of-Body Travel*. New York: HarperCollins, 1996.

————. *The Secret of the Soul: Using Out-of-Body Experiences to Understand Our True Nature*. New York: HarperCollins, 2001.

Gallenberger, Joseph. *Brothers Forever: An Unexpected Journey Beyond Death*. Charlottesville, Virginia: Hampton Roads Publishing Co., 1996.

Garfield, Patricia. *Pathway to Ecstasy: The Way of the Dream Mandala*. New York: Holt, Rinehart, and Winston, 1979.

Greenhouse, Herbert B. *The Astral Journey*. New York: Avon Books, 1974.

Harary, Keith, and Pamela Weintraub. *Have an Out-of-Body Experience in 30 Days: The Free Flight Program*. New York: St. Martin's Press, 1989.

Hughes, Marilyn. *Odysseys of Light: Adventures in Out-of-Body Travel*. Norfolk, Virginia: Hampton Roads Publishing Co., 1991.

————. *Crystal River Flowing.* Norfolk, Virginia: Hampton Roads Publishing Co., 1993.

LaBerge, Stephen, and Howard Rheingold. *Lucid Dreaming: The Power of Being Awake and Aware in Your Dreams.* New York: Ballantine Books, 1985.

————. *Exploring the World of Lucid Dreaming.* New York: Ballantine Books, 1990.

Leland, Kurt. *Otherwhere: A Field Guide to Non-Physical Reality for the Out-of-Body Traveler.* Charlottesville, Virginia: Hampton Roads Publishing Co., 2001.

————. *The Unanswered Question.* Charlottesville, Virginia: Hampton Roads Publishing Co., 2003.

McCoy, Edain. *Astral Projection for Beginners.* St. Paul, Minnesota: Llewellyn Publications, 1999.

Moen, Bruce. *Voyages into the Unknown.* Charlottesville, Virginia: Hampton Roads Publishing Co., 1997.

————. *Voyage Beyond Doubt.* Charlottesville, Virginia: Hampton Roads Publishing Co., 1998.

————. *Voyage into the Afterlife.* Charlottesville, Virginia: Hampton Roads Publishing Co., 1999.

————. *Voyage to Curiosity's Father.* Charlottesville, Virginia: Hampton Roads Publishing Co., 2001.

Monroe, Robert. *Journeys Out of the Body.* New York: Doubleday Books, 1971.

————. *Far Journeys.* New York: Doubleday Books, 1987.

————. *Ultimate Journey.* New York: Doubleday Books, 1994.

Moss, Robert. *Conscious Dreaming: A Spiritual Path for Everyday Life.* New York: Three Rivers Press, 1996.

Muldoon, Sylvan, and Hereward Carrington. *The Projection of the Astral Body.* York Beach, Maine: Samuel Weiser, Inc., 1929, 1973.

————. *The Phenomena of Astral Projection.* York Beach, Maine: Samuel Weiser, Inc., 1951, 1972.

Peterson, Robert. *Out-of-Body Experiences: How to Have Them and What to Expect.* Charlottesville, Virginia: Hampton Roads Publishing Co, 1997.

————. *Lessons Out of the Body: A Journal of Spiritual Growth and Out-of-Body Travel.* Charlottesville, Virginia: Hampton Roads Publishing Co, 2001.

Taylor, Albert. *Soul Traveler: A Guide to Out-of-Body Experiences and the Wonders Beyond.* Covina, California: Verity Press, 1996.

Van Dam, Vee. *The Psychic Explorer.* London: Skoob Books Publishing, 1989.

Weor, Samael Aun. *Logos Mantram Theurgy.* Los Angeles, California: The Gnostic Association, 1987.

Wilson, Terrill. *How I Learned Soul Travel.* Golden Valley, Minnesota: Illuminated Way Publishing, Inc., 1987.

About the Author

Preston Dennett grew up very skeptical of all things paranormal. He graduated from University of California at Northridge with a bachelor of arts in English and found employment as an accountant. In 1984, following the death of his mother, he saw her ghost and experienced a series of dream visitations from her spirit. Still skeptical, he reluctantly began to research various paranormal phenomena. He studied shamanism, UFOs, dreams, ghosts, life after death and eventually out-of-body experiences.

Intrigued by the idea of going out of body, he decided to try the exercises. To his shock, he easily slipped out of his body, and after much trial and error, learned to control the ability. He has since had hundreds of OBEs and has made many advanced explorations into the astral dimensions.

Today, Dennett is a leading UFO researcher and ghost hunter, and has authored five books and more than eighty articles covering the full range of the paranormal. He has appeared on numerous television and radio programs. His research was featured in the *Los Angeles Times* and Los Angeles's *Daily News*. He has taught classes on out-of-body experiences and has lectured widely across the United States. He currently lives in Canoga Park, California.